Walking in the Light

A Seeker's Guide to Spiritual Development

Tracey Howarth Tomlinson

2QT Limited (Publishing)

2QT Limited (Publishing)
Settle
North Yorkshire
BD24 9RH
United Kingdom

Cover image: Zoran Karapancev/Shutterstock

Printed by IngramSparks UK Limited

A CIP catalogue record for this book is available
from the British Library

ISBN 978-1-912014-13-2

Medical Disclaimer

The information provided in this book is designed to provide helpful information and not intended to replace any medical advice nor does it offer any diagnosis or treatment for medical conditions. The publisher and author are not responsible for any specific health or allergy needs that may require medical supervision and are not liable for any damages or negative consequences from any treatment, action, application or preparation, to any person reading or following the information in this book.

Therefore if you have any health/mental health problems, or if you are currently taking medications of any sort, you should consult your doctor or equivalent health professional prior to undertaking any of the suggestions in this book. Reading this book does not establish a therapist-patient relationship.

References are provided for informational purposes only and do not constitute endorsement of any websites or other sources. Readers should be aware that the websites listed in this book may change.

This book is dedicated to all the people in my life who have assisted me in my life's journey. It is dedicated to my husband Mark and his unwavering belief in me. To my sons Conor and Joshua, thank you for your patience while writing and thank you for choosing me to be your mother in this incarnation. I am so proud of you both. To my dad, from whom I have learnt so much and who made me the person I am today, and to my stepmum Janet, for being a strength and for teaching me about strong women. To Jackie, for continually encouraging me to keep fit and for keeping me grounded. To my friend Carl, for his words of wisdom and encouragement. To my spiritual teachers Julie Atkins and Yvonne Smith, who changed my life and set me firmly on my path, I am forever grateful. To all my friends and family, for without you I wouldn't be here.

Contents

Chapter 5

Chapter 6

Chapter 11

Chapter 12

Bibliography and Further Reading

Introduction

As far back as I remember I have always seen spirit. In many ways I was a withdrawn and shy child. A lot of my shyness was due to the upheaval I experienced when I was young. As a child I would often awake to see someone sitting on my bed. When I sat bolt upright to touch them, they disappeared. I think at the time I told my father, and he would reply that it was just a dream. I knew it was something else. As startling as it sounds, I was never afraid, and still to this day I occasionally wake up to some being sitting on my bed, although it doesn't happen as much now.

I was awkward as a youngster, quite different to how I am now. One day in school, during a religious education lesson, the teacher told us that we could speak to God at any time. I was so lonely it seemed like a revelation – speaking to an invisible friend, that is. So, I began speaking to God every day on the way to school. I don't think he (or she) ever replied, but this was the start of my connection to the spirit world, in that I had the knowledge that there were unseen helpers who could assist me on my path.

The event that truly changed my life was attending

an angel workshop in 2010. I was at my lowest ebb and had been attending spiritual development classes with Julie, who was a medium. She was holding an angel awareness class and encouraged me to come along.

I had always been aware of angels. As a Roman Catholic they were easy for me to accept. I always believed that I had a guardian angel, that we all have guardian angels.

During that workshop I experienced massive changes. I connected with the angelic realm in a way I had never known before. I felt such love and peace that I felt as if I was floating in an eternal paradise. Everyone in the group saw my transformation. Even my face changed. The lines of stress and anxiety that I had been feeling seemed to melt away. My energy had been lifted, and I felt that I had tuned into an alternative vibrational frequency.

Despite the ups and downs of life I know that the angels and guides are with me constantly, as I have learnt not to grasp at things but let go and let them guide me. When fear of the future or the pain of the past grips me I focus on the present moment and go into a state of allowing, knowing that I am fulfilling my destiny. Over the years the realisation has dawned on me that life is a journey and not a destination. All we are left with at the end of the day are memories, so we should make as many happy ones as possible.

My spiritual journey started many years ago, but that one day in the angel workshop really accelerated my spiritual path in life. I stepped on to and off the spiritual path along the way, but life's experiences tended to shove me right back where I should have been all along. And life has a habit of doing this. Life's experiences put you exactly on the path where you are meant to be in life.

It is through experiencing the presence of angels, fairies and unseen helpers that one may become aware that realms may exist beyond our normal day-to-day comprehension. Some may say it is an escape from reality, a dream world. Perhaps what we perceive as reality is the actual illusion. It doesn't matter hold young or how old you are. Life holds such wonder and mystery that you just need to tap into it.

Every day can hold new wonder and excitement. Tapping into unseen forces can help smooth our path in life and perhaps make our way that little bit easier. It isn't about losing a grip on reality, but about allowing an alternate reality to coexist within our own. It's about getting in touch with our true nature, with our spirituality, and to live our lives in harmony with one another and with nature.

To heal our bodies we first need to heal our thoughts. Fears, anxieties and stress can all play a part in bringing our physical bodies into dis-ease. This dis-ease may eventually lead to physical illnesses.

How do we turn this around? Firstly we need to quieten our mind. By tuning our thoughts to love, peace and humility and by living in the now we can train our mind to let go of fears and anxious thoughts. By connecting with God, the divine (whatever you wish to call it), and surrendering our thoughts to God or the universe (again, whichever you prefer), we can connect with the inner essence of love, peace and light of our being.

Ask for guidance and it will come. It may come through an urge to do something, for example, to purchase a book, or it may come by way of a friend's wise words. So if you are struggling to connect to divine guidance, the message here is to ask. Put it out into the universe and the message will come through to you if you believe that it will.

When we are in fear and hate we live within the ego self. The ego self will trick us into believing that we are above others, that we can't do things that we want to do to improve our lives or that we need addictive substances with which to cope with life. The ego can put you into a poverty mindset or a mindset of the eternal victim. The ego is not just about arrogance, greed or stubbornness. The ego can build us up as well as knock us down.

Much of today's society is fear-based. We live in an age where we can access news, stories and videos in an instant. It is my belief that the people in control of the media and politics feed fear to the masses in order to exert control. When did you last switch on the news and see a story that gave you hope? That warmed your heart?

We need to be mindful and alert to the negative images that we are bombarded with each day. We need to be mindful of our thoughts and actions, and not fall into the trap of engaging in other people's fears or dramas. Simply acknowledge them and move on.

Do not be drawn into gossiping or ridiculing others but remain calm, focused, loving and centred.

Changing our thoughts and deeds may not happen overnight. It may be a long process. We tend to forget ourselves and momentarily end up getting drawn into other people's actions. There may be anger that arises during the day because someone has wronged you, or the gossiping that you just can't help but join in with.

These are the negative energies that you may encounter during the day, along with the stresses and strains of everyday living, the worry about when the next wage is coming in or the rising cost of living.

The Earth plane is one of learning. When someone angers or ridicules us, we must ask, 'What is it teaching us? What lesson can we learn from this?'

Before we were born into this life we chose what incarnation we would take. We chose what experiences we would have. We are experiencing exactly what we are meant to experience, and it is all part of a divine plan. Everything that we experience is what is meant to be. What we mustn't do is to sink into the dark depths of despair, but instead we must turn towards the light and have the knowledge that everything is being reflected back to us in divine, eternal truth.

We all have our own path to tread in this life. It is up to us to make our life as peaceful and as loving as possible. This doesn't mean becoming a doormat in life, but it means lovingly standing in our own power and having no fear about what anyone else thinks of us.

Invite God and the angels into your life. Ask for

forgiveness for any mistakes you feel that you have made. Ask to be released from pain and guilt and for your life to be made better. When the realisation hits that everything is for a purpose and that the purpose is to learn and move on, those lessons hopefully come into perspective. You will not dwell on them as much but instead acknowledge them and let them go.

Forgiveness is the key in healing emotions. When we are in conflict with our emotional state, we enter into anger, hate, fear, loss and feelings of betrayal. To forgive others for their actions is to release their grip on our lives. We can then take steps to fill this void with love, peace and kindness.

Unforgiveness manifests in the body as dis-ease. It can manifest in the physical through various ailments. It is well known that stress can manifest into the physical body and present itself through various conditions, and unforgiveness and anger can also have the same effect. They are all negative emotions. When we place ourselves on the path of peace we transmute all negative energies and place ourselves on the path of wellness and wholeness.

We can look upon the words of the Ho'oponopono, a mantra of forgiveness:

I love you… I'm sorry… Please forgive me… Thank you.

The belief behind this mantra is that any anger or hatred or fear that we hold in our emotions manifests into the physical by way of dis-ease of the body. Or it manifests in negative emotional states, by way of discord and disharmony showing up in our daily lives, by way of things not running smoothly and by having arguments or upsets. By reciting this mantra you can bring your thoughts back to those of peace. It's amazing how effective it is, and it can be used in any situation and at any time to bring harmony to the mind.

When we are at peace within ourselves we are at peace with the world around us. There are those who we encounter in life who thrive on anger, hate, discord and disharmony. That is because they do not understand their true nature or their authentic selves, and they are lost in the vacuum of fear and anger. Sometimes these people see those of a spiritual nature as a threat. They embrace the fear and discord in their lives because they know no other way. They may not understand peace and harmony if they have never experienced it in their lives themselves.

It may be that we cannot change the mindsets of these people, but we do have the power to change ourselves and to lead by example. To honour the peaceful, loving part of ourselves is to embrace our true nature and to step on to the path of peace, happiness and abundance. It means to be in the moment and to not worry about what has passed, nor to fret about what the future holds. Be in the now, and allow others to be who they want to be. Assert yourself in a loving manner, but do not force your views on others. Only when an individual is ready can they choose to change their mindset to one of peace and harmony and leave pain and anger behind.

This book is a culmination of everything that I have

learnt over the past twenty years. It is a selection of tools and exercises that can help you develop your spiritual path and empower you. Over the years I have read a lot of material and attended many workshops and learnt a lot along the way.

I have put together some exercises, meditations and tools to help you connect with the unseen world of spirits, fairies and angels, to work on your chakras and bring your body into alignment.

You may wish to purchase a journal to record your experiences with any of the meditations and exercises within the book. Journaling will help record your development, and can be kept for later reflection to see how far you have progressed.

Once you understand that the physical life you experience can be enhanced by a greater knowledge and understanding of the spiritual world, you will create a better life for yourself – a world of peace, harmony and abundance. You have the power within you to create the life you truly want.

Chapter 1

Meditation as a Tool for Healing

'If you want to conquer the anxiety of life, live in the moment, live in the breath.'
Amit Ray

In 1997 I found myself with quite severe depression after the birth of my youngest son. At the time we had a shop. Although it was what we wanted, the overheads were crippling us and we found it hard, working seven days a week. We had no money and debts were piling up. We had very little support from the family and my mother-in-law was a severe alcoholic drinking a litre and a half of sherry a day, sometimes more.

I felt like I was in a deep, dark pit with no way of crawling out. It was a heavy shadow cast over my life and I never thought I would see the light again. All I wanted was for someone to take care and look after me but I felt alone, helpless and desperate. Life just wasn't meant to be like this, I thought. I had never cried as much in my life. My husband found it hard to cope. It was the darkest time of our lives. I sought help and started to see the psychiatrist at the local hospital. It was when he suggested that I go into hospital and my sons be put into foster care that I really sat up and took notice of how bad things had got.

I loved my boys so much I couldn't bear to see them taken away from me. That's when I made the decision to take charge of the situation and help myself. I'd got myself into this mess and I would get myself out of it.

I thought back and remembered how I'd done some meditation a few years back. The depression was clouding my judgement and I needed clarity of thought. I was walking around daily with a thick fog in my head that I needed to shift. I knew that meditation and not medication could heal my mind. I was consuming antidepressant tablets and breastfeeding my baby. What effect was this having on his health? Once my mind was healed I knew that I could start taking action steps to claim back some quality of life for all of us.

I started to meditate as much as I could. It was difficult in the mornings with the baby but I found that 9 p.m. was my optimum time, when the boys were in bed. I would use deep breathing techniques to get myself calm and focus on my breath.

After time I began to feel better. I noticed that my panic attacks began to subside. I soon realised that the deep breathing techniques that I had practised at night could be used to help alleviate my panic attacks. After a few weeks my panic attacks began to disappear.

When I began to feel the benefits of my meditation

and deep breathing practice, I stopped taking my medication. Although we were still struggling to pay the bills and still working hard, the fog in my head began to fade bit by bit. I now felt that I could start to take charge of my life once again. We decided to close the business. It happened quite fast, and I arranged for someone to come and buy all the stock. We still had an agreement to pay the rent for another six months.

I knew that somehow we would get the money to pay. I believed that the money was coming somehow and that we would be all right, even though Mark and I were out of work. We both found work quite quickly. I began waitressing and Mark found temporary warehousing work. Then, after spending most nights praying that we would see the end to our problems, our prayers were answered when the landlords terminated our tenancy agreement, which meant that we didn't need to pay any more rent. The relief I felt on hearing the news was enormous. It was as if a weight had been lifted off my shoulders. We finally felt that we could take charge of our lives once more. My worst fears of ending up bankrupt were finally fading away. It was like a miracle.

I continued my meditation practice and began to get back to normal. By the time my son was two I felt the depression finally lift. I used positive affirmations every day, saying to myself, 'Every day in every way I am feeling better and better.'

My prayers were eventually answered as I got better. I'd come through the darkest time of my life, and came out the other side. To this day I look back and give thanks because the depression forced me to take stock and change my life for the better. I began to take courses at college and train as a holistic therapist, and went from strength to strength. My life at this time still wasn't perfect. I had to work hard to pay my debts. We had to live with the threat of a visit from the bailiffs for an overdue tax demand. However, we coped, and I put all my effort into paying our debts off. Eventually, after two years of continually watching the pennies, we became solvent and could actually look at moving house. By this time I had a job at a local college which I loved, and my husband landed a job with the Post Office. Although not perfect (what is?), we now finally had the sort of life we deserved.

I continue to meditate most days. It has helped me greatly in times of stress, especially when I was teaching, which was an extremely demanding job. The meditation I do now has helped me develop my intuition and enhanced my ability to act as a channel for healing.

How Meditation Works

Meditation is a great tool in helping to reverse the effects of stress and in calming the mind and the emotions. When under threat the adrenal glands release certain hormones so that the body can prepare for the flight or fight response. This in turn causes the muscles to tense and the blood pressure to increase, making our heart beat more intensely and making our breathing become faster and shallower. As I mentioned before, I had quite severe panic attacks. This was in part my body's reaction to stress; part of my own fight or flight response. This response is part of our ancestral make-up, and originates from when we had to run from wild animals or run away at times of real danger. In today's life some people find that this response is provoked not only at times of real danger but also when people are faced with what they perceive as stressful situations.

During meditation, the brainwaves alter to a distinctive alpha pattern. While meditating, one can experience enhanced mental awareness while simultaneously feeling a deep relaxation.

People who regularly meditate can move into this mode at will. This allows them to counter stress more efficiently and helps lower the blood pressure and combat muscle pain. When I felt that things were overwhelming me I would regularly go to the bathroom and take a few moments to breathe deeply and get into the zone. I now do this merely by thinking, 'Peace.'

Meditation is the key to spiritual and psychic development, but it is also key to calming our mind and our emotions and is excellent for relieving stress. Stress creates a fog over our mind so that we cannot see or perceive situations with clarity, and it clouds our judgement. Meditation helps to lift this fog so that we can see situations as they really are and react to them in a calmer and more positive manner.

When your mind and body are calm you can access

your intuition and your imagination, and these are where your hopes, dreams and creativity come from. When you can access this source of creativity and wisdom you will find that you will be able to attract what you want in life more easily. You will also be clearer about what you want to attract and create in your life.

My life has moved on greatly from where I once was. If you'd have seen me then and looked at me now you would think that we were two different people. Even my own family members, when asked, would never have believed that I would have come on as far in life as I have. It has taken time, patience and persistence. It has not been easy. Meditation for me has been the key for my development, and it can be for you too. However, this does not mean we need to be Buddhist monks in order to achieve the calmness and well-being that meditation can bring. Meditation is, after all, an acquired skill that you need to persevere with. Meditation can come in many forms.

Becoming More Aware

Through the act of meditation one naturally becomes more spiritually aware. As the mind slows down and the awareness shifts, one can tap into the level of consciousness that exists outside the physical realm. There are many layers to the consciousness that exists outside the physical realm. When you awaken spiritually from the slumber of everyday life you become more aware of the endless possibilities, and of the existence of many different dimensions.

When you realise this, the possibilities are endless. No longer will you be stuck with the humdrum of life, but you will realise that you are able to create your own reality, one that fits with your view of how the world should be. You will be able to create in your life everything that you feel you need. In this, though, one needs to be mindful of the grasping ego. We must create from a spiritual want, not from just a materialistic viewpoint.

To be truly spiritually awakened is to be aware of the endless possibilities that exist in the universe. There are many realms that exist, including galactic energies. As with all meditation practice the key here is intent. We must be of the mindset of attracting to ourselves that which is pure and of 100 per cent light, of love and of truth. In this way we energetically enhance our lives in a positive way. Once your energetic vibration lifts, you attract into life that which is of positive vibration. As you become more spiritually aware the things that you once held dear may naturally fall away. Your circle of friends may change as you seek out those of a similar mindset. Your dietary requirements may change as you decide to eat and drink more high-vibration foods and beverages. You may even be less interested in television or the news than you once were. These are all signs of a shift in consciousness and of an alteration in your vibration.

Once the realisation that everything is an illusion hits, you realise that you can create your own reality. The only thing that will stand in your way is your own ego. The ego may put up resistances by holding on to fear-based energies such as alcohol, drugs or cigarettes, chocolate, poor food choices or other addictions. These will fall away when one is ready. Ask your angels and spirit guides to help you in your quest. Intent is the key.

Simple Meditation Exercise

Find a quiet place where you will not be disturbed. Unplug the phone; switch the mobile off. Sit or lie comfortably. I prefer to sit, as this way I know I won't go to sleep. If you are sitting, make sure your feet are flat on the floor. If they are not, place a cushion or a book under your feet. Close your eyes and take a nice deep breath.

Focus on your feet. Visualise roots sprouting from your feet, anchoring you to the earth and grounding you. Draw up through these roots the energy of the earth, which will empower you and help to clear away all negative energy.

Now begin to focus on your breath. Take a deep breath in. When you breathe out, imagine all the stresses and strains of the day melting away. Breathe in and feel that you are breathing in peace and relaxation. Breathe out and see all the tension and worries melt away.

As you continue to breathe in, imagine that you are breathing in a pure white light. As you breathe out, imagine you are breathing out a grey mist. The grey mist is all the tension, worry, problems and niggles you may have encountered during the day.

Sit in this peace for five or ten minutes. If your mind wanders, bring it back to focus on your breathing. Focus on your chest, gently lifting up and down as you breathe. Focus on the beat of your heart as it pumps the blood around your body. Acknowledge any thoughts that arise and see them float away into the ether.

When you are done, feel at peace and fully relaxed. If you can, try to do this for twenty minutes daily. But remember that even five minutes is better than no minutes.

At the end of your practice, surround yourself with a translucent bubble to help seal in the peace and to protect yourself from negative emotions. Be of joy and positivity and give thanks for the experience. See the bubble expand fifteen feet below you, fifteen feet above you and fifteen feet from each side of you and fill it with love, light and peace.

Try to do this practice daily. You will be amazed at the benefits it will have on your health and well-being. There will be times when you do this practice that your mind keeps wandering. This is normal, so don't be put off. Perseverance is the key.

Variations

Meditation comes in many forms. The above meditation can be done in the same way, but by using a candle. This is called a focus meditation. It may help you if you find your mind continually wandering.

Light a candle at the beginning of your meditation practice. Close your eyes. Use your breathing to breathe away tensions. See roots emerge from the soles of your feet and ground you to the earth. Breathe in the white light of peace and positivity and breathe away the grey mist of stress and negativity. When you are relaxed, open your eyes and gaze gently at the candle. Think of nothing else but the flickering flame. Soften your focus and hold the image of the flame. Close your eyes and allow nothing else to enter your mind. If your mind wanders, open your eyes and gently focus on the flame. Continue focusing on the flame, and then close your eyes for as long as you can. If you can manage it, aim for at least twenty minutes. Seal and protect your aura in a translucent bubble as before.

You may find this meditation practice easier than concentrating on the breath. Eventually, after doing this meditation a number of times, you will be able to simply visualise the candle. As a precautionary note, please always take care with candles and make sure you extinguish them properly after use. Use candles safely and don't light them near curtains or anything combustible. You can also consider using an electric candle, but please be mindful of the environment if you have to dispose of it. In my mind natural candles are always the best, due to their natural light, but it is up to preference.

Another type of meditation is the walking meditation.

While walking outdoors, bring your attention to your feet. As you walk, feel each footstep one in front of the other. As you walk, imagine all the tension and stress of the day flowing from your body and leaving through the soles of your feet. Imagine the negativity that flows out of your feet leaves footsteps behind you that transform into beautiful flowers. Breathe in the white light of peace and see the negativity continually flowing out of your feet as you walk. Continue in this way for as long as you feel necessary.

It is important while doing this meditation that you feel safe; I don't advise it near busy roads. It is a good meditation to do, though, in parks or in the countryside or even in your garden. Connecting with the outdoors and the earth are always good for getting rid of anxieties.

From this you can see that there are many ways of doing meditation. My husband likes to fish, and will spend many hours staring at a float. This, in a way, is a focus meditation. He feels the immense benefit of sitting for hours in the countryside staring at his float, and always comes home relaxed and at peace. Many people enjoy golf for a similar reason: the outdoors, the green of the grass, the trees and concentrating on a small ball as it is knocked about the golf course. Running or jogging can also be considered a meditation. In fact, any exercise is good for getting rid of the toxins and negativity accumulated during the day. I always find time to exercise during the week by doing aerobics and strength training. I am not thin, but I am healthy in mind and body. The two go hand in hand.

There are many variations that you can use in your meditation practice. There are numerous albums of meditation music you can purchase. If you listen to music while meditating, please ensure it has no words. Meditation is very powerful, and words can have a subliminal effect on the psyche. For this reason it is best not to meditate to music that contains words. However, if you wish you can purchase guided meditations. Guided meditations are where you are talked through a journey, and at the end you should feel peaceful and relaxed.

Whenever you meditate, always visualise roots coming from the soles of your feet and grounding you to the earth. This to my mind is important, as it keeps you connected to the earth, especially when you are opening yourself up to higher consciousness. If you don't ground yourself during meditation you may feel out of touch with reality once your meditation practice is complete.

There is also a wealth of groups and meditation circles that you can join. In the UK there are many Buddhist meditation groups that welcome new members. There are also many meditation groups run by individuals and at spiritualist churches. Check online, look in your local directory or enquire at your local spiritualist church or Buddhist centre.

White Light Meditation

Find a quiet place where you will not be disturbed. Sit in a comfortable position. It is better to do this meditation sitting upright rather than lying down, as the energies will travel through the top of your head and through the body. You may wish to burn a candle and/or incense.

Close your eyes. Take a deep breath. As you breathe in, imagine breathing in peace. On the out breath, breathe away all tension and anxiety. Breathe in peace and love. Breathe out all tension, stresses and strains. As you breathe in, imagine all the tensions of the day and any thoughts and fears melting away with the out breath.

Continue to breathe in and out in this way until you feel calm and relaxed. Now, begin to imagine a pure crystalline or white light above your head. This white light is pure and full of love and peace.

Breathe in this white light through the top of your head. As it enters your head, feel it melt away all thoughts and fears, leaving your mind still and peaceful. Breathe out.

As you continue to gently breathe in and out feel the white light moving down the back of your head, making your head relaxed. Feel the white light moving over your eyes and face, making all the muscles relaxed.

As you continue to breathe, feel the white light now moving down your neck, through your shoulders, making them relaxed. Now feel the light travel down your arms as it travels down your fingers and thumbs, taking all tension with it, leaving your arms feeling relaxed.

Now take this light from your shoulders down through your spine as it travels through your trunk, relaxing all the muscles and organs as it goes through your body.

Feel the light now travel down over your hips, through your thighs, knees, calves and ankles and out through the heels of your feet, leaving your whole body calm, relaxed and at peace.

Feel roots now, growing from the soles of your feet, down into the earth, anchoring and grounding you. Feel these roots grow and expand deep into the earth, like the roots of an oak tree, firm and strong. As these roots go deep into the earth they find a crystal and the roots wrap themselves around this crystal.

Now draw the pure energy from the crystal back up through the soles of your feet, through your ankles, calves, knees and hips.

Feel the energy from the crystal move up through your trunk, stomach, chest and internal organs as it travels up your spine to the base of your head. Take the energy of the crystal across your shoulders and down through your fingers and thumbs.

Now feel the crystal energy move up through your head as it moves to your crown (the top of your head). Feel this energy flow out through the top of your head as it now begins to flow outwards, filling your energy field with pure, crystalline energy. Feel it filling and expanding through your energy field at arm's length *all around your body.*

Sit in this energy feeling peaceful, relaxed and healthy for a few minutes. If your mind wanders at all, focus on the gentle rise and fall of your breath.

Now begin to bring yourself back. Feel the streaming of the white light disconnect. Feel yourself sitting in the chair. Move your fingers and toes and feel aware of your surroundings.

When you feel ready, seal and protect this wonderful energy within your own energy field. Clench your fists and imagine a sphere of protection fifteen feet below you, above you, in front of you, behind you and at both sides, all around you like a huge translucent bubble, protecting you and keeping you safe. To finish, if you can, reach down and put your palms on the top of your feet to ground yourself. If you can't reach that far just run your palms down your legs as far as they will go. Stay there for a few seconds, then sit up and open your eyes.

Task: Meditation Practice

Try to meditate daily. Find a time that is suitable for you. You may prefer meditating in the morning, as I do, or in the evening when the kids are in bed. Try to do at least ten minutes a day, ideally twenty minutes daily. Always remember to see the roots developing from your feet and grounding you. Record your experiences and how it makes you feel in your journal.

Chapter 2

Understanding the Chakras

*'What we feel and think and are is to a great extent
determined by the state of our ductless glands and
viscera.'*
Aldous Huxley

The Chakras and the Subtle Bodies

When developing our intuition and our psychic and
healing abilities we need to understand the chakra
system and how it works. By the process of meditation
and mindfulness we bring the chakras into balance
naturally. By knowing the functions of the chakras
we can understand the imbalances that manifest in
the emotional and physical bodies. We also need to
understand the chakras as a point of healing ourselves
and, if we choose to, others. Harmonious and well-
balanced centres create a well-balanced individual.

The word 'chakra' comes from the Sanskrit word

meaning 'wheel'. They are considered to be centres of prana, life force or energy, and are considered to be energy centres within the human body. This is a simplified, basic interpretation of the chakra system.

The chakras are part of the subtle bodies, which are in turn a part of the human energy field or aura. The human body consists of a series of subtle bodies. Each of the subtle bodies is a field of energy that vibrates at different rates of frequencies within the aura. These are, briefly: the physical, the emotional or astral body, the mental and then the causal body.

Collectively these subtle bodies form part of what we know as the aura. Psychics may be able to clairvoyantly 'see' these fields emanating from the body, but most people will not be able to physically see them. The idea that the body emanates with an invisible energy field has been a long-held ancient belief. With the development of Kirlian photography, the reality of its existence may be established. Regardless of differing views on the subtle bodies, it is clear that the human body is more than just the physical elements you can touch. The emotions and human consciousness (thought processes) are also parts of the human make-up. These contribute to the overall well-being of a person. It is well known, for example, that stressful lives can play a huge part in the development of physical illness. Information about these subtle bodies and about the chakras can be found in ancient Indian yogic literature. The subtle bodies emanate from the chakras and work in unison with one another.

The Chakra System

Each chakra corresponds to vital organs within the body, and each is associated with a particular colour. The body contains many chakras but there are seven main chakras, which are connected by ethereal threads to the body via the spinal column and head .

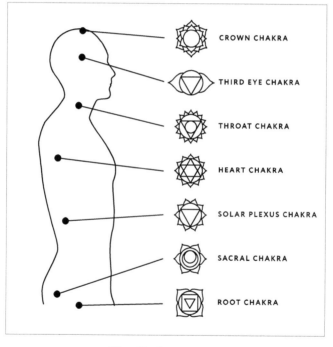

CROWN CHAKRA

THIRD EYE CHAKRA

THROAT CHAKRA

HEART CHAKRA

SOLAR PLEXUS CHAKRA

SACRAL CHAKRA

ROOT CHAKRA

The Chakra system

The Base Chakra

This is situated in the perineum, between the anus and the genitals. In Sanskrit the name for this chakra is muladhara, meaning 'base' or 'root'. It represents the will to survive. The colour red and the element of earth are both associated with this chakra. This chakra is unlike the others as it faces downwards, connecting our subtle bodies to the earth. The adrenal glands are associated with this chakra. The adrenal glands are responsible for the flight or fight response in humans in that they prepare the body for action by the production of adrenalin.

The dormant power of the kundalini resides in this area. When the kundalini is awakened it rises up through the chakra system. It is likened to a snake rising through the body. When it rises it is said to bring enlightenment with it.

In the physical body this chakra rules the bones, the feet, the legs and the large intestines. Imbalances in this chakra can show in the physical as constipation, obesity, sciatica and haemorrhoids. At an emotional level, imbalances can be in the form of grief, depression and instability as well as extreme self-centredness and greed.

The Sacral Chakra

This chakra is situated in the midpoint between the pubis and the navel. It presides over procreation, sexuality and creativity. In women it includes the womb. This chakra also presides over all liquids, blood, urine, menstrual flow and seminal fluids and is also connected with the kidney and the bladder. Imbalances with this chakra can cause problems with these functions.

When this chakra is awakened it can promote increased psychic abilities and improved intuition. The sex drive can be affected either in a positive or a negative way when working with this chakra, but this should settle down eventually. It is the centre of control and is associated with power, money and sex. When it is out of balance it can show up as addictions, jealousies and poor relationships.

The colour associated with this chakra is orange, and it is said to work closely with the base and the solar plexus chakras, as it is between them. It is associated with the element of water.

The Solar Plexus Chakra

The solar plexus chakra correlates to the area of the pancreas. Its colour is yellow and it is associated with the element of fire. It is the centre of personal power. The body parts it governs are the digestive system, the stomach, the small intestine, the spleen and the liver.

This chakra gives us a sense of empowerment. When our will is blocked we can sense a tightening of the solar plexus area. An example of this would be when we are frustrated or anxious. When the emotions are suppressed they remain held in this chakra until they are unleashed, which may be in the form of an emotional scene, a crisis or a breakdown. Anger can be stuck in the solar plexus for a long time.

Nervousness, anxiety, fear or butterflies in the stomach are part of the mirroring of this chakra in action. When one awakens this chakra it is said that one can master fire, an example of which is psychic heat.

The Heart Chakra

The colour of this chakra is green and it is associated with the element of air. It is linked above the heart in the region of the thymus gland. It reflects the emotions, as the image of the heart represents the area of love. It is the centre of emotional power. The body parts it governs are the lungs, the heart, the arms and the hands.

When fully stimulated, this chakra can give us inspired speech and eloquence. It can also help develop poetry, but it is not easy to awaken. It is the centre of love, but our experience of love may be limited to family, friends, children and others who, in return, love us equally.

The sense of touch may be heightened with the opening of this centre. The ability to heal may be made stronger as we work on this chakra.

When this chakra is out of balance it may show in the physical body as heart disease, asthma, lung disease or high blood pressure. Emotionally it may express itself as greed, lack of tolerance, insincerity and the inability to receive love. Or it may express itself as racism or sexism. This chakra is about being able to love freely without fear, and the tolerance and acceptance of all living things.

The Throat Chakra

This is the centre of will and choice. Its colour is bright blue and the element associated with this chakra is ether. It relates to communication, creativity and listening. The body parts it governs are the neck and shoulder areas. When it is out of balance there may be a fear of speaking, a difficulty in expressing feelings, shyness, a weakness of the voice, being tone deaf, having no rhythm, gossiping or too much talking.

On the physical level it may manifest as a sore throat, thyroid imbalances, colds or swollen glands and respiratory problems. This chakra is also assigned to the function of hearing as well as telepathy and channelling. When the throat chakra is not active one's creative ability will be diminished. When it is activated, one will have the ability to see the past, the present and the future.

The Brow Chakra

The brow chakra is the centre of intellect and reasoning; the power of the mind. Its colour is indigo and it is not associated with any element. It is situated on the brow, just above the bridge of the nose. This centre, when awakened, acts as a third eye. Powers of visualisation – the ability to see via the mind's eye - are increased when this chakra is activated. The body parts it governs are the eyes and both hemispheres of the brain.

This chakra is linked at the pituitary gland (there is much debate over whether it is linked to the pineal or the pituitary). Its purpose is to help us 'see' our life's path and therefore fulfil our spiritual purpose. We do this through our inner vision and intuition. We can develop clairvoyance and insight and learn from life's lessons. When this chakra is activated, the ability to visualise may increase. Visualisation is a key element in meditation, self-healing and psychic development. When it is out of balance it can manifest as headaches or nightmares, or may affect the vision. Denial, delusions or being afraid of one's intuition may also manifest as a result of any imbalances.

The Crown Chakra

This is the centre for mysticism and grace. It is where you experience a connection to the divine and the development of wisdom. Its colour is violet and it is not associated with any element. It is situated at the crown of the head. It is connected to the physical body via the pineal gland (although there is debate about this).

The body part it governs is the brain, in particular the cerebral cortex, and also the whole body.

This is the last of the seven major chakras. The crown of the head is extremely sensitive, and the chakra resides four finger breadths from the top of the head. The opening of this chakra, through devoting oneself to spiritual development and meditation, may take a long time – perhaps even many lifetimes. Traditionally, painting of saints and ascended masters such as Jesus are portrayed with a halo around the head, which is a representation of the fully awakened crown chakra.

If we devote ourselves to spiritual development the crown chakra will open slowly. When one does not undertake spiritual development this chakra can remain dormant.

Once this chakra is fully awakened there is enlightenment and ascension to the higher realms. The soul, once enlightened, will have no more need for reincarnation and will be free from being reborn in a future life.

When this chakra is opened we experience connection to the spiritual self and experience wisdom, thoughtfulness, awareness and understanding. When it is out of balance it may manifest as migraines, delusions, brain tumours in the physical body and comas. On an emotional level we may experience greed, materialism, or exert domination over others, or we may have rigid belief systems or difficulties in learning.

The Chakra Meditation

Find a quiet place to sit where you will not be disturbed. Turn off the phone. If you wish you can light a candle or some incense or put on some soft music. Do whatever makes you feel happy.

Sit with your feet flat on the ground. Close your eyes. Take a few slow, deep breaths. As you do this, start to connect with the universal white light of the divine consciousness. Breathe in this white light as you have done before, in the white light meditation.

Visualise a shaft of pure crystalline white light

coming down from the cosmos and entering the top of your head. See it engulfing your body inside and out, leaving through the soles of your feet and cleansing all negative energies as it travels through your body.

When you have breathed in the white light, concentrate on the soles of your feet. See roots like those of a tree sink deep into the earth, grounding and anchoring you.

Now see the energy move through your body as it reaches your base chakra, situated in your perineum. Breathe in the colour red. As you breathe in the colour red, see your chakra become balanced with a red hue. If you see any muddiness or imbalance, breathe it away.

Next, take the energy to the lower abdominal area, the sacral chakra situated below your belly button. Breathe in the colour orange. As you breathe in the colour orange, see your chakra become balanced with an orange hue. If you see any muddiness or imbalance, breathe it away.

Visualise the energy now travel to the solar plexus chakra situated above your belly button and below your chest. Breathe in golden yellow. As you breathe in the colour yellow, see your chakra become balanced with a yellow hue. If you see any muddiness or imbalance, breathe it away.

When you are ready, shift the energy and breathe it into the heart chakra situated in your chest. Visualise in a bright green and see it expanding with loving radiance. As you breathe in the colour green, see your chakra become balanced with a green hue. If you see any muddiness or imbalance, breathe it away.

Now move towards to the area of the throat. Breathe the energy up to the chakra situated in the throat. Breathe in the colour blue. See it emanating, a bright blue, from the centre of the throat. As you breathe in the colour blue, see your chakra become balanced with a blue hue. If you see any muddiness or imbalance, breathe it away.

Next, take the energy to the third eye chakra situated on the bridge of your nose. Breathe in the colour indigo. As you breathe in the colour indigo, see your chakra become balanced with an indigo hue. If you see any muddiness or imbalance, breathe it away.

Move your attention to the top of your head. Breathe the energy into the crown of your head, where the crown chakra is situated. Breathe in the colour indigo. As you breathe in the colour indigo, see your chakra become balanced with an indigo hue. If you see any muddiness or imbalance, breathe it away.

Now sit for a few moments as you feel all your chakras balanced and aligned.

Finally, visualise breathing in the pure crystalline white light which surrounds you from head to toe in every direction, flooding your entire organism inside and out. Protect your energies within a bubble of light.

Feel your whole body healthy, balanced, aligned and refreshed. Open your eyes when you are ready. Stretch and touch your feet to ground yourself.

Try this meditation and make a note in your journal of how it makes you feel. You can complete this meditation regularly to clear and cleanse your chakra centres.

Task: Making an Auragram

For this exercise you will need paper, crayons (the easiest medium to use for this exercise) or coloured pencils, and another person to sit for you.

Sit opposite the other person with the paper in front of you and the crayons to hand. Close your eyes and take a few deep breaths. Tune into the other person's energy field with your eyes still closed.

When you are ready, gently open your eyes and hold a soft gaze over the person sitting opposite. What colours come to mind for this person? Begin to work this colour on to the paper. Are there other colours? Are there any shapes? Try not to think too hard about it. Let yourself go with the flow as you develop your aura-gram. Once you are finished you can interpret your aura-gram for the other person. What did the colours say to you? Were they happy, vibrant, solemn, energetic or random?

You will be surprised at the way the images and colours come and how you interpret them. With practice this exercise will get easier, especially if you struggle at first. The trick is to just let it flow.

This exercise is fun to do and helps to develop your creative nature.

Chapter 3

Connecting with Spirit Guides and Helpers

'All I have seen teaches me to trust the Creator for all I have not seen.'
Ralph Waldo Emerson

Spirit guides are those unseen helpers who guide us throughout our life. They are responsible for ensuring that we fulfil the contract we took on when we incarnated into this life. We are all assigned a spirit guide to help us on our journey. Whether we are aware of our guides or not is another matter. These spirit guides come in many different forms. Some spirit guides will be around us for a lifetime, and some spirit guides will come into our lives to help with a particular task when needed. When I was developing spiritually I found that my guides changed constantly. This was because I was developing quickly and my guides changed in order to bring through the new energies that I was emerging with.

As the consciousness evolves and develops through

the practice of meditation, awareness of the connection to the spirit realm and higher states of consciousness will become easier and more apparent. Through developing our awareness the brain will begin to work in different ways. It will shift from more left-brain thinking to more right-brain creative thinking. When communication from the spirit realm comes through, you may question whether or not it is real communication, or if it is your imagination. The key word here is trust. You must trust that the messages you are receiving are from higher realms and are not just your ego. It is important to put your ego aside and clear your mind as a vessel for such communication. Without a clear mind the messages won't come through with much clarity. Of course, some people, as with everything, will find it easier than others. The answer is perseverance. Yet, at the same time, don't try too hard. Just being in the moment and not straining to receive messages is vital.

The key to connecting with the higher realms is intent. If you wish to receive messages from spirit, and have the intent, then these messages will come to you. The images you receive may be subtle and may come by way of symbolism. With practice you will be able to decipher these and develop the knowledge of what the symbols mean.

There are many places where you can develop mediumship. Spiritualist churches run development circles where you can develop under the guidance of an experienced medium. Many mediums run their own development groups and workshops. It is much easier to find out information now, through the Internet and via social networking sites. Again, ask for guidance from spirit and they will put you in touch with the right people. In England there are many spiritualist churches up and down the country and they can be your first point of call if you're struggling. And don't forget meditation circles, as you will find many like-minded people with whom you can connect.

It took me many years to find the right spiritual teachers. I found my spiritual teacher in a cafe in my local town. The front of the premises was a cafe and a coffee shop, but in the back Julie conducted development circles, past life regression and psychic suppers. She opened up a whole new world to me. From one of the members in the group I then came in touch with Yvonne, who taught me healing and working with the angelic realm. Julie's teachings were practical and down-to-earth and Yvonne's were very highly spiritual and angelic, but both were equally gifted and talented in the way they worked. So, I'd waited years for the right teachers of the craft and two came along at once. The point of this is that the right teachers will appear at the right time and not before. Again, put the message out there into the ether and have patience.

So, what do I mean by using the term connecting to higher dimensions? Mediums only connect to the deceased, don't they?

When you open yourself up spiritually you open yourself up to the possibility of connecting with many other realities and dimensions, not just the realm of the deceased. The spiritual realms exist on many different layers and expand higher and higher to the God consciousness or the divine, whatever you wish to call it. These dimensions are given through my interpretation of how they exist and are touched on briefly. Your belief systems may develop differently as you progress spiritually.

The realm of spirit, of deceased loved ones, exists just beyond our own conscious mind. Contact can be made with this realm through raising your vibration. Meditation is the tool for the practice of raising your vibration. Mediumship or spiritual development circles under the guidance of an experienced medium can help you develop further. The spirit realm itself is layered, as some who pass over into spirit are more highly evolved than others. Some who pass into spirit are not aware they are dead. Some who pass into spirit are not aware of God. Others are. Deceased loved ones who pass into spirit may keep elements of their personality which may be spiritual, gentle, boisterous or domineering. As on the Earth plane, there are opportunities for those in the spirit realm to learn and develop further. Some in spirit will take up a commitment to assist those on the Earth plane by way of becoming a spirit guide. Some may evolve higher spiritually. Some may not.

Beyond the spirit realm exists the realm of the ascended masters. These are people who have evolved so highly on the spiritual plane that they no longer need to reincarnate on to our physical plane. They have lived through incarnations and have learnt their earthly lessons. They have acquired wisdom and mastery beyond the physical realm and have freed themselves of karma. They are enlightened individuals who have had a physical incarnation. Saint Germain, Jesus and El Morya are examples of ascended masters. Again, the realm of ascended masters sits on many layers, as each evolves differently to another and brings with them various teachings and influences. If you wish to learn more you may be interested in reading some of the many books on ascended masters, such as those by Madame Blavatsky and Alice Bailey.

Beyond the realm of the ascended masters is the angelic realm. The topic of angels could take up a whole book, but we will look at them briefly in a later chapter. This realm also exists in various layers or hierarchies, from those angels closest to the physical realm to those closest to God. All the realms have within them light and dark entities. As with all higher work in any of the realms, and when connecting to spiritual entities, it is vital that you request entities of one hundred per cent light – the most highly evolved entities that you can work with. Ask any energies or entities that do not feel good, or not of the light, to move away. As with all work on the energetic level, intent is a key element.

Task: Meditation to Meet the Spirit Realm

Find a quiet space where you will not be disturbed. Make sure the phone is off the hook/switched off. Have your journal and pen ready to make notes at the end. You may like to light a candle and/or burn incense. Sit or lie comfortably and close your eyes. Begin to take nice deep breaths.

As you breathe in, imagine breathing in peace. On the out breath, breathe away all tension and anxiety. Breathe in peace and love. Breathe out all tension, stresses and strains. As you breathe in, imagine all the tensions of the day and any thoughts and fears melting away with the out breath. As you breathe in again, breathe the white light through the top of your head and into your body. This white light clears away all stresses, strains and worries. As you breathe out, imagine all these stresses, strains and worries leaving your body. Breathe in and out this way until you feel relaxed and at peace.

Turn your attention to the soles of your feet. Visualise roots coming out of the soles of your feet, like the roots of a tree, connecting you deeply to the earth, grounding you, ready for your journey.

See yourself going through a tunnel. It is a long tunnel but you are not fearful, because at the end of the tunnel you see a beautiful white light. You know that the white light at the end is peaceful and loving.

As you emerge out of the tunnel, you find yourself in a beautiful garden. It has beautiful flowers and wonderful aromas. You see butterflies dancing in the dappled sunlight. You take time to look around at all the beauty that there is in this garden. Take a few moments to look around.

You find a path in this garden. It leads off into the distance through the garden. All you can see are endless flowers and plants on either edge of the path. As you walk along the path, you are greeted by your guide. Even if you do not fully see your guide you are aware of their presence. Your guide is happy to see you and full of love for you. You greet your guide and together you walk the path through the garden.

At the end of the garden path you find a wooden door set in a high stone wall. You open the wooden door and you find yourself in a field full of grass. You walk through the field and feel the grass beneath your feet. The field of grass leads to a bridge. Take a moment to look at the bridge.

On the other side of the bridge you see a group of people. As you look at the group of people you will see some familiar faces. They are people that are no longer in the physical realm. They are waiting eagerly for you to cross the bridge and greet them. They are full of love for you and your guide. You have no fear, only love. Your guide takes your hand and you cross the bridge together.

When you get to the other side a familiar face makes their way to the front of the crowd to greet you. You take a few moments to listen to what they have to say. If you wish, you may ask questions. You listen to the conversation and know that you will remember it later.

When you are ready, you thank the person for this time together. Your guide takes you by the hand and leads you back over the bridge. You walk through the field of grass as you approach the high stone wall that holds the wooden door.

You open the wooden door and close it behind you. You are now in the beautiful garden once more. You look around the garden one last time, taking in the sights and smells as you and your guide walk the garden path together. You see the tunnel in the distance. You turn and thank your guide and say goodbye for now. You know that your guide will always be there for you.

You walk to the tunnel and enter it. You walk through the tunnel to the light at the end. As you emerge from the tunnel you come back into the room, back to your quiet place.

Breathe deeply and bring yourself back to full awareness. Wriggle your toes and fingers. Run your hands down your legs and, if you can, touch your feet to ground yourself. Stretch if you want to. Open your eyes when you are ready. Get your journal and pen and write down everything you can remember.

Spirit Guides

Spirit guides come in many forms. They may appear in a form that is relevant to your life's path. For example, some spirit guides will appear as monks or Native Americans to bring that essence of their being and understanding to you. This is why many spiritual people appear to have guides in these forms: the guides will appear in a way that you can understand.

The spirit guides are different from our higher selves. Our higher self will be constant throughout our lives. The higher self is the connection of us to the

God consciousness and so doesn't alter throughout our life. The higher self can be compared to our soul as it travels through lifetimes.

Spirit guides are different in that they may change according to the individual's spiritual need at the time. When I first started meditating many years ago, my spirit guides appeared as Native Americans in their native dress. However, over time my spiritual guides became more Middle Eastern in appearance and more ancient – biblical, almost.

Seeing your spirit guides should not, however, be the be-all and end-all. I was absolutely desperate to see and speak to my spirit guides for many years. When eventually, during a meditation, I communed with my spirit guide, he told me some very profound things that I didn't understand. When I looked up what he had told me I was taken aback. There was no way that I would have known about the information he gave. I had to research the information, and all that he had told me was correct. The information given was so profound that, had I received the communication prior to that moment, I would never have understood it. So it is wise to know that spirit guides will show themselves and communicate with you only when you are ready spiritually, and not before.

True spirit guides will come to you in a loving, peaceful way. The energy will feel light and comforting. When guidance comes through you may feel a tingling sensation, a light pressure on your head; you may feel the energy shift inside your auric field. True spiritual guidance will make you feel uplifted.

If the energy or messages you are receiving do not feel loving or peaceful, please ask that spirit to leave. When I connect with spirit guides I say a small prayer and ask that I be connected only with those beings of 100 per cent light and for my highest good. Ask that the guidance comes from the highest source possible, closest to God. The key here, as with all light working, is intent. Focus on peace and love when connecting to ensure that you only attract the highest, most positive and most loving vibrations.

When connecting with spirit guides, make sure you have your journal at hand to write down any messages or images.

Meditation to Meet Your Spirit Guide

Find a quiet space where you will not be disturbed. Make sure the phone is off the hook/switched off. Have your journal and pen ready to make notes at the end. You may like to light a candle and/or burn incense. Sit or lie comfortably and close your eyes. Begin to take nice deep breaths.

As you breathe in, imagine breathing in peace. On the out breath breathe away all tension and anxiety. Breathe in peace and love. Breathe out all tension, stresses and strains. As you breathe in, imagine all the tensions of the day and any thoughts and fears melting away with the out breath. As you breathe in again, breathe the white light through the top of your head and into your body. This white light clears away all stresses, strains and worries. As you breathe out, imagine all these stresses strains and worries leaving your body. Breathe in and out this way until you feel relaxed and at peace.

See roots like the roots of a tree coming out of the soles of your feet. These roots go deep, deep into the earth, grounding you ready for your journey.

See ahead of you a tunnel. As you enter this tunnel you feel no fear. The tunnel is dimly lit. At the end of the tunnel you see a bright light. You head towards this bright light at the end of the tunnel.

As you emerge out of the tunnel you find yourself in field of long grass. You walk through the field, feeling the softness of the earth and grass beneath your feet. You feel the long grass with your hand as you continue walking. You smell the fresh clean air and feel the sun shining on your face. You feel a gentle breeze in the air. You hear the birds sing in the distance. You pass by a stream gently gurgling to your right. You stop for a moment and listen to the gentle sound of the water passing over the rocks and stones.

Ahead of you is a hill with gentle grassy slopes reaching upwards. You walk up this hill with ease. As you get to the top you see a circle of stones. You know that this is an ancient circle of stones and it feels peaceful and loving. You make your way into the circle of stones. As you look all around there are mountains emerging in the distance. It is a beautiful place, and you are overjoyed at the beauty and peace that you experiencing.

As you turn to face where you entered the stone circle you see someone approaching. It is your guide.

You have waited a long time to see your guide and now they are here. Take a moment to look at your guide's appearance. What are they wearing? How does your guide appear?

Your guide has much love for you and is overjoyed that you are here to greet them. You and your guide embrace each other briefly. You take a moment to look into your guide's eyes. They are gentle and hold much wisdom and knowledge. You know that they are going to pass on this wisdom and knowledge to you.

You begin to talk. Don't worry if you can't hear the words immediately. Just know that the conversation is being had. You may receive thoughts and images as well as words. You take a few moments to listen to your guide's loving and gentle words of wisdom and guidance.

When you have taken time to listen you may ask a question. You wait and listen for the answer. Don't worry if the answer doesn't come immediately. Just know that the answer is being given. You stay here and listen for a while as your guide speaks to you.

The time is ready for you to end your journey. You thank your guide for the wisdom and knowledge they have imparted. You are very grateful for this experience. You and your guide embrace and say your goodbyes. You know that your guide will always be near you and that you can come back to this place any time you wish.

You go back thorough the entrance of the stone circle and make your way down the gentle grassy slope of the hill. You reach the field and make your way through it, feeling the grass beneath your feet. You run your hands through the grass as you go. You pass the stream, which is now to your left. You take one last look at the scenery all around you.

You see the tunnel and enter it. It is still dimly lit and you see the light at the end. You emerge out of the tunnel to find yourself in your quiet place. You come back to into yourself. Breathe deeply and bring yourself back to full awareness. Wriggle your toes and fingers. Run your hands down your legs and if you can, touch your feet to ground yourself. Stretch if you want to.

Open your eyes when you are ready. Get your journal and pen and write down everything you can remember.

The Four 'Clairs'

When we are developing and opening up psychically we will receive information from the spirit realms in different ways. It is necessary to understand these different ways of receiving information metaphysically, as not everyone possesses the ability of clairvoyance or clairaudience. When you are starting out to develop spiritually you will probably receive your information as sensing intuitively or just knowing. This is why it is important to trust the information you are receiving, as it is very easy to doubt yourself or just put it down to sheer imagination.

Clairvoyance – this literally means 'clear seeing'. This is when a medium can see a spirit, or receives a vision of something that is about a happening or a situation.

Clairaudience – this means 'clear hearing'. This is when a medium can hear spirit. They receive information through an inner or outer voice.

Clairsentience – this means 'clear sensing'. This is when a medium senses information rather than hearing or seeing it.

Claircognizance – this means 'clear knowing'. This is when a medium just knows the information but hasn't had the information relayed through any other source.

The Higher Self

The higher self is an extension of you. It is separate from your ego. When the ego takes over the human condition one's higher guidance will become diminished. This is why some people seem more highly connected than others, and why some receive higher guidance more clearly. It is all down to the ego.

The higher self coexists alongside the ego, but is separate. The higher self is a reflection of the true spiritual nature of your being. It has been by your side through past lives and will be with you constantly through this lifetime. When you fully connect with the higher self, clear spiritual guidance will unfold. The higher self will guide you to situations, people and a lifestyle that will reflect your true spiritual nature and help set you free from the limitations of everyday life. This is what is meant by synchronicity. When you are on the correct life's path and in tune with your higher self, events will develop in a synchronistic way and coincidences will happen that are meaningful. Life will be clearer, and not bound by the ego.

It is when we live our life dominated by the ego that our lives can seem disjointed, desperate, unhappy and unsatisfactory. Our ego tells us we need a bigger house, a better car or a more beautiful partner. When we connect with the higher self, the want and desire for these things will naturally diminish, and we will be set on to the path of happiness.

The higher self is not a departed loved one or a guardian angel. The higher self is the essence of your being. It is your connection or channel to the divine or to God. When you access the higher self, you tap into your soul's purpose in this lifetime. Your higher self may come through to you by way of thoughts and impulses that are not ego-based.

Connection to higher guidance can be done simply by intention. If it is your intention to connect with higher guidance it will happen. The key to strengthening the connection is to focus on lessening the ego. When you connect with the higher self you will have a deep sense of knowing. Remember that the higher self is not separate but is part of you.

Meditation will further enhance the connection to the higher self.

Connecting with the higher self is the first step

to connecting with other realms of existence, such as the spiritual and angelic realm. There are many planes of existence apart from the physical one that we experience on the Earth plane. For some, the thought that there are other planes of existence may be difficult to understand, but we must free our mind to the possibilities. We understand our world by sight and touch, but many planes of existence can be tapped into by the power of thought.

The higher self exists just beyond the physical, etheric, mental and emotional bands of our being. The physical part of us is the first. Then there is the etheric body, the interface between the physical and the higher bands. Then there is the mental band: our thoughts. Then there is the emotional band: our feelings. Just beyond these bands exists the higher self. There is a lot of information available on the subtle bodies, as they are known. But, for now, this is all we need to know.

Once we connect with the higher self we can move on to connecting with higher spiritual realms. Connecting with the higher self is the first important step and will guide us along our path. One way is to make a note of our dreams. Communication with the higher self may come through our dreams when we are asleep.

Begin to take note of your dreams and write them down in a journal. Journaling is an excellent way to connect with the higher self. Write down your thoughts and feelings regularly, as well as your dreams. This is a good way to connect to your higher guidance. As you write things may come to you from your higher guidance.

Also try the white light meditation. This will help you connect to the divine source or God, which in turn will connect you to your higher self. There is no need to attach a persona to your higher self. Just allow it to be there. However, your higher self may appear to you as a male or female person, and this may be to help you develop your understanding. My higher self just is. I know it is there and it exists. It has no form except being, and I know that it is a constant part of me, separate from the ego.

Task: Giving a Spirit Reading

For your first reading, try to read for someone who will be supportive and patient. Also remember to be patient and calm with yourself. Don't try to force the reading, as this will be counterproductive.

Sit or stand, with the person you are giving the reading to sitting in front of you.

Begin by getting yourself into a meditative state. You may wish to draw down the white light by breathing and drawing the white light through the top of your head.

Call in your guides to assist you with this reading.

You are now ready to give your reading. You may feel spirits drawing near. As you communicate with them, be clear that you only have their attention during the course of the reading and give clear, positive messages to the person you are reading for.

Say what impressions come to you. Do you have an impression in your mind? Do you hear a voice? Do you see anything? Is it male or female? Fat or thin? What is their hair like? Their facial features? Do they have a name? Do they have a special message for this person?

Try not to pose questions to the person who is sitting for you. It is better to trust in the process and relay the information given to you from the spirit world. In this way you can test the reliability of the information given and know that has not just come from your own ego. This in turn helps to develop confidence in your abilities.

When you have finished give thanks to the spirit and guides and to the person that you have given the reading to. Ask the person sitting for you for some positive feedback. You may want to write your experiences in your journal for later reflection.

Chapter 4

Angelic Connections

'For he will command his angels concerning you to guard you in all your ways. On their hands they will bear you up, lest you strike your foot against a stone.'
Psalm 91: 11-12

After developing my mediumship skills with Julie, she asked if I would like to do a one-day angel workshop with her. I wasn't really sure, but I thought I'd give it a go. In the Roman Catholic faith we'd been brought up to believe that we were assigned a guardian angel who would look after us for the whole of our earthly life, so I didn't entirely dismiss the existence of angels but I still thought that they were just biblical myths. Whenever anyone spoke to me about angels I tended to switch off. I'd forgotten about them.

I turned up to Julie's class on a Sunday in February 2011. It was cold, wet and miserable, and I felt equally miserable too. My husband and I were struggling with the death of my mother-in-law, who I was very close to. There was so much going on that I really needed a boost. Really I was just hoping that we'd do some nice meditations that might uplift my spirits. I certainly wasn't expecting anything more.

Julie engaged the group with various meditations through the day to connect with the angels, and it really is difficult to put into words what the energy felt like. I really connected to the angelic realm, and I when I walked home at the end of the day I felt as if I was floating. I can honestly say that from that day on my life changed dramatically. My relationship with my husband Mark improved considerably. I even asked the angels to help me, ahead of a difficult meeting with management at work, and it went smoothly.

The week after the workshop I was guided to make an angel altar. I needed an angel, some gold cloth and a gold candle. I found an angel straight away that I had seen in an angel article I was reading. Next I had a look round for a gold candle. I stopped and asked the angels to guide me to a gold candle. I received a vision in my head of a shop that was just out of the town centre that I hadn't been to for years. I walked in and there on the shelf was a gold candle sitting there on the shelf on its own.

Amazed that I had received the guidance with such clarity, I asked the angels to guide me to some gold cloth or something similar to cover my table. I was guided back to the town centre, to the market and to a fabric stall. There in front of me were offcuts of cloth and, lo and behold, there were rolls of gold lamé-style cloth. I went home and made my altar, using the objects that had been guided to me with the addition of a few of my crystals.

But then a few days later something happened that really reinforced the idea that the presence of the angels was not to be doubted by my rational mind. I decided to look for a book that I thought may be in the attic. I climbed up the ladders to the loft space and lifted the hatch. I poked my head through the opening and there, right in front of my eyes, face down, was a small fabric angel in gold and cream – an old Christmas decoration. It was not one that I had ever seen before. Nor had I ever seen it in the attic before, and we had lived there for eight years. That little angel sits on my table to this day as a reminder of the angels and the beautiful ways they can come into your life.

After this I had the same repeated thought coming into my head … to take up healing again. Only this time it was to be angelic healing. I had no idea if there was such a thing as angelic healing. My friend Alison, who was part of Julie's development group, suggested I see her reiki teacher, Yvonne. Meeting her changed my life once more. She had developed her own form of reiki, incorporating the angels, and called it angelic Usui reiki. She had such a deep connection to the angels, and helped me deepen my connection with them too. She taught me how to bring the angelic energies into a healing and as a result many of my healing sessions have been very profound, both for me and for the receiver.

When you invite the angels into your life your life can change in many ways for the better. They are always by your side, ready to assist. All you need to do is ask.

Connecting with Angels

When we think of angels they are immediately by our side. There are no special rituals that we have to complete for the angels to be by our side. Just think of them and they will be there. We connect to the angels through our hearts and minds.

In order to hear angelic communication more clearly we need to work on raising our vibration. This can be done by consuming high-vibrational foods and beverages. Eating a mainly plant-based diet, staying away from alcohol, drugs and caffeine – and exercising regularly – all assist. Connecting with nature frequently by being out in the fresh air and in open spaces also raises our energies. Meditation and yoga are other ways to raise our vibration.

So there are many ways in which we can raise our vibrational energies. Do what you are guided to do and remember that taking small steps to change your lifestyle can make a huge difference.

Messengers of God

The angels are messengers of God, and as such we do not worship them. There are many different hierarchies of angels and hundreds, if not thousands, of angels. For the purposes of this book we will concentrate on the archangels.

Each archangel brings with them a special virtue or quality. They are the connections of humans to the divine consciousness or God. Their role in life is to bring peace and God's will to those who open their hearts to the angels. They cannot, however, interfere with one's free will choices. It is up to the individual to ask for the help of the angels. These requests must be made from the heart and be of good intent. They will help guide and protect you in positive ways. All you need to do is ask.

The angels may influence your mind by thought. There may be recurring thoughts that encourage you to do something, something that you asked for being suddenly put in your path or subtle voices speaking to you. Or, as is most common when angelic communication begins, there may be symbols. These symbols can be recorded in your journal and you may want to interpret possible meanings behind any symbols you receive.

When you begin working with the angelic realm, I feel it is easier to work with the major archangels. By definition, these are high-ranking angels. The archangels can be found in religious texts, mainly those from Judaism, Christianity and Islam. They are non-denominational and omnipresent, which means that you can call on them to assist at any time. You will not be taking them away from essential tasks, as they can be in many places at once.

We all have what is called free will. The angels cannot help us unless they are asked. If you ask your angels for help you are not taking them away from important missions, no matter how trivial your request may be.

A good example is the car parking angel. The next time you go somewhere in the car, ask your angels for a car parking space to be available for you when you get to your destination. You could use the request, 'Please help me, angels, to find the perfect car parking space in which to park my car easily.' When I remembered, I used to ask for a car parking space to be available on Saturday afternoons in town when I took my invalid mother-in-law shopping, when car parking spaces would invariably be few and far between. More often than not a car parking space would be available on the busiest of days.

The angels can be asked for things that will be of benefit to our highest nature. We cannot, however, ask the angels to interfere with another person's free will. Nor will it work if you ask them for Saturday night's lottery numbers. It just doesn't work like that. We can, however, ask for things that make our lives happy and peaceful, for things that are for the good of ourselves and others. Angels cannot be summoned to do anything that is not at one with good or God's light. Nor must we worship them, as they are purely God's helpers and messengers. Instead we give all the glory to God, the divine, or whatever name you identify with most closely. Angels act on God's behalf by bringing peace to the world, and this is their divine mission. When we live our life in a more peaceful way we are more in tune with our authentic self.

The realm of the archangels is the easiest that the human consciousness can tap into.

The angels will influence you by thought. Ways in

which the angelic realm may be working with you can include having recurring thoughts that encourage you to do something, or perhaps something that you have asked for is suddenly put in your path. Or you may even hear subtle and loving voices speaking to you.

When I first started working with the archangels I would ask for and receive a symbol. This symbol could be anything from an apple or a book to a deeper religious symbol. One morning I was given what looked like a ship's wheel and I did not know what it meant. I looked it up on the Internet to find it was in actual fact the Tibetan wheel of life. Then I meditated on the symbol, and my meditation became very deep and in turn gave me insights into how I could improve my life and what changes I had to make.

The archangels lead many other lesser angels in their work. They are all working in conjunction with God's will and for the benefit of humankind. For the beginner, it is always best to work with the archangels initially, as they are easier to commune with. As with all work with the spiritual realms, the energies you work with should be loving and positive. If it does not feel right, ask it to leave. Always ask to work with beings of pure, loving light.

You may call upon the angels to assist with any situation at any time. You will not be taking them away from any other work as they are omnipotent: that is, they can be in multiple locations at the same time.

You can request the help of the angels with all sorts of situations in your everyday life. The most common problem areas in our life are our relationships, our career, our family life and issues surrounding our finances. However, the angels cannot work against the free will of others. This means that you cannot use the angels to coerce other people against their free will, such as make them fall in love with you.

You can, however, ask the angels for help and guidance for the highest good of yourself and others. The angels will hear your request and work their magic. The end result might not be what you expect but may be something even better, which you hadn't even thought of.

This is the key. What you expect is not necessarily what you get in the way you think you will get it.

An example of this is from my personal experience. On two occasions many years ago, I asked the universe and the angels to send me a new car. On both occasions my cars were stolen. I did get new cars, but not in the way I expected. And it had to happen twice, because obviously I hadn't learnt my lesson the first time. It's not that the angels or the universe wanted me to suffer, because they did grant me what I asked for. But if I'd have put my request another way by using a more positive affirmation the results may have been different.

So, instead of just asking for a new car, a better way would be this:

'I thank God and the angels for my new car, which I can easily afford, and which is for the highest good of all.'

When using affirmations such as this, always keep them in the present, give thanks and finish it off with, 'For the highest good of all,' as this acts as your insurance policy to make sure that it comes to you through positive actions.

Another example may be a relationship that you have had with someone has turned sour. Perhaps it could be a disagreement with a colleague or a family member who has upset you, or someone has jumped to the wrong conclusion or misjudged you in some way. An affirmation can be made to help send peace to the situation, such as:

'I thank God and the angels for assisting me in this situation in a peaceful and loving way, for the highest good of all.'

In this way there are no exceptions, no demands. It leaves it open for the angels to work their magic in the best way possible, and unconditionally.

Another example is when we repeatedly tell ourselves that we are short of money. We tend to continually affirm that we are struggling by saying, 'I'm broke, I have no money, and I can't afford it.'

Instead we could use more positive words such as, 'I thank God and the angels for the wonderful abundance that is manifesting in my life now, for the highest good of all,' or, 'I thank God and the angels for guiding prosperity to me at every turn, for the highest good of all.'

Or maybe we need help with finding a job or hitting those sales targets:

'I thank God and the angels for all the opportunities that are manifesting in my life now and the abundance that they bring for the highest good of all.'

Keep it simple, keep it in the present, always give thanks as if you already have it and keep it unconditional. Most importantly, finish it off with, 'For the highest good of all.' In this way you are making sure that it is for the benefit of everyone around you and will not interfere with the free will choices of others. You may even say, 'This or something better,' in your affirmations. You may change the word 'angels' and use the name of a specific angel to help with a problem. For example, Archangel Raphael is the healing angel. I ask him specifically to assist with any healing work I do, and I ask Archangel Gabriel to help with communicating my ideas or delivering a teaching session. The list is endless. Use the angels to enhance all areas of your life and experience the joy that they bring.

The sphere of the angels is the closest to the human realm, and within this sphere are the guardian angels. They have the ability to access all the other angels. They deliver our prayers to God and deliver answers back. The archangels exist in a higher realm to the angels.

We will look at each archangel in turn.

The Major Archangels

In this section we will look the major archangels. Although we associate each angel with a feminine or masculine aspect, angels really are neither. The terms 'his' or 'her' are used for each angel, but you can decide for yourself.

Archangel Ariel

Her name means 'lion or lioness' of God. When she is near you may experience visions of lions, and she is also associated with the wind. She oversees watery environments, as well as the protection and healing of nature. She helps with the protection of wild animals and works closely with Archangel Raphael to heal animals. You may sense a change or breeze in the air when she is with you. She can be called upon to assist in environmental matters when nature is in danger, such as developments on greenfield sites. She works closely with the fairy realm and the elemental realm. She can help manifest with earthly needs, such as help with finances.

Archangel Azrael

His name means 'God helps'. His aim is to assist people at the time of their passing. He also helps people to cope with their grief. Azrael can be called upon to comfort those who are dying and to help with their crossing over. His energy is believed to be quiet, comforting and composed. He guides souls to the kingdom of heaven. Azrael will also help you find the answers you to questions that you may have, and also to find trust and faith.

Archangel Chamuel

His name means 'One who sees God'. He is considered to be a peaceful healer of relationships. He is also considered a leader of the heavenly hierarchy known as the powers. As such, he protects the world from lower energies and protects us from those who wish to control the world in negative ways. He can also help protect our personal world. He can be called upon to help us find lost items that are physical as well as non-physical things such as our life purpose, our relationships or our careers. He can help you find the things that you are seeking in your life, such as the right place to live, your soulmate or whatever you are seeking.

Archangel Gabriel

His name means 'God is my strength'. His symbol is the trumpet. This angel is one of the most familiar, and he was the angel who told Mary of the future birth of Jesus. He is therefore known as the messenger angel. He assists with the adoption or the conception of children. He can also help anyone whose life purpose involves art or communication, such as actors, singers, writers, teachers or dancers. Those who deliver spiritual messages can also call upon this angel. Gabriel is the angel of positive action, and those who ask for his assistance will be pushed forwards into positive action. In the sacred circle, Archangel Gabriel resides in the western quarter and is associated with the element of water.

Archangel Haniel

Her name means 'glory of God'. She is associated with the moon and the planet Venus. The ancient Babylonians called upon her to assist in divination and healing work. She will help with clairvoyance and intuition. She helps find natural healing remedies and assists in channelling the energy of the moon in potions and crystals. You can call upon Haniel to add the company of wonderful friends to your life. She will help you answer your prayers and be receptive enough to receive those answers. She can add grace, harmony and beauty to our lives. She helps with feminine issues such as menstrual cycles, PMS and the menopause.

Archangel Jeremiel

Jeremiel's name means 'mercy of God'. Calling upon Jeremiel can help when you are experiencing difficult times, and he will help you to see through situations. He helps you to forgive yourself and others. He helps us work with karma and releasing old patterns in life that are holding us back. He helps to put us back on the right path according to God's will, and to let go of regrets.

Archangel Jophiel

This angel's name means 'beauty of God'. Traditionally known as the patron of artists, she was present in the Garden of Eden, according to biblical texts. She helps us see the beauty around us and to think beautiful thoughts. She can also be called upon to beautify our words and deeds, and to generally beautify our lives. She helps with creative and artistic endeavours, and can help beautify the spoken and written word. Calling upon her can help turn around unpleasant situations.

Archangel Metatron

The meaning of Metatron's name is not known. He is believed to be one of only two mortals who became angels (the other is Sandalphon). He is sometimes called the angel of presence. He is considered the youngest of the archangels because of his previous earthly existence, having lived his life as Enoch, who was a prophet and a scribe. He received the Sefer Raziel HaMalakh (the Book of Raziel the Angel). This book was said to be created by Archangel Raziel which was given to Adam, Noah, Enoch and finally Solomon.

Enoch ascended as an angel to the highest level to live and work. He keeps records of everything on Earth and stores it in the Akashic records. Having once experienced an earthly life, he acts as an intermediary between Earth and Heaven and assists those who are in their earthly existence. He assists children, helping them to develop spiritual gifts, as well as helping those who have crossed over. He can also help newly developed people in deepening their spiritual gifts. When you call upon him he will help you in making bold choices and will give you motivation. Archangel Metatron stands above the sacred circle.

Archangel Michael

His name means 'he who is like God'. He is in charge of the order of angels known as the order of the virtues. He inspires light workers to carry out healing and spiritual work. He can assist in conjunction with Archangel Raphael with healing work.

He taught Adam to farm in the Garden of Eden and purportedly gave courage to Joan of Arc to lead France during the Hundred Years War. He is said to appear as tall, handsome and carrying a sword. He uses his sword to set us free of fear and to cut etheric cords of attachment. When he is present you may see flashes of purple or bright blue. He can also be called upon to fix mechanical and electrical devices. He can be called upon to guide you to your life's direction, purpose or career path. He is also regarded as the patron saint of the police. He can motivate and guide us and help us to increase our self-esteem. He can also be called upon to help us overcome addictions. Archangel Michael stands in the southern quarter of the sacred circle and presides over the element of fire. He is the archangel of the summer solstice.

Archangel Raguel

This angel's name means 'friend of God'. He assists with developing harmonious relationships. He oversees all the other archangels and angels and ensures that they are working harmoniously together. He is often referred to as the archangel of justice and fairness. He helps those who are doubted or trodden upon, to give them self-respect and empowerment. You can call upon him to resolve conflicts and to act as a mediator.

Archangel Raphael

This angel's name means 'God heals'. He is a powerful healer of animals and people. Raphael can be called upon on behalf of others, but, as with all other angels, cannot interfere with another person's free will. Raphael is also known as the patron of travellers, as he travelled with Tobias in the Book of Tobit and kept him free from harm. He helps with all aspects of travel as well as spiritual journeys.

Tobias was shown by Raphael how to use fish parts in medicinal ways. Raphael can guide healers during treatments. He helps with the education of would-be healers and helps in setting up their practices by attracting clients. He is a guide and healer for all animals. He can often work in conjunction with Archangel Michael to guide lower energies away from people and places. He helps with addictions, clairvoyance, space clearing and spiritual release. His presence may be indicated if you see flashes of emerald green. Archangel Raphael stands in the eastern quarter of the sacred circle and presides over the element of air.

Archangel Raziel

This angel's name means 'Secret of God'. This is because he is reputed to know the secrets of the universe. He created the Book of Raziel the Angel (see also Archangel Metatron). The origins of the book have been heavily debated by scholars, but the book itself is difficult to understand and it is said that one must call upon Archangel Raziel in order to understand it.

This angel can assist in revealing to you secret esoteric knowledge. He can assist in the understanding of high-level knowledge, such as sacred geometry and quantum physics. He can help with your ability to access divine guidance. Calling upon him can help you deepen your spiritual practices and the understanding of them.

Archangel Sandalphon

This angel's name means 'brother' in Greek in reference to his 'twin' brother, Archangel Metatron, both of whom were originally mortal men. Sandalphon, in his earthly incarnation, was the prophet Elijah. Immortal assignments were given to both men for their earthly good work. Elijah was ascended to the heavenly realms in a fiery chariot led by two horses of fire, according to the Bible.

Sandalphon's main role is to take human prayers to

God to be answered. He is said to extend from Earth to Heaven, as he is so tall. His messages may come to you as soft whispers or as music in your mind. He can be called upon to assist with music and creative endeavours. Archangel Sandalphon stands at the bottom of the sacred circle.

Archangel Uriel

This angel's name means 'God is light'. He shines his light on situations or may give prophetic messages. He is the angel of wisdom and intelligence. He warned Noah of the flood, assisted the prophet Ezra to predict the coming of the Messiah and gave the Kabbalah to mankind. He is regarded as the wisest of the archangels, and will give practical insights and solutions to problems. Uriel's assistance can be called upon when the weather or earth events affect us, such as earthquakes, tornadoes, floods or any other natural disaster. He can also be called upon to assist with writing. Archangel Uriel stands in the northern quarter of the sacred circle and presides over the element of earth.

Archangel Zadkiel

This angel's name means 'the righteousness of God'. He can help you feel mercy and compassion towards yourself and others. He helps facilitate forgiveness and helps us see the divine light in everyone. He can help with our remembering our life's purpose. He can be called upon to assist in memorising information, or with assisting your memory in general.

The Divine Circle

The angels of the divine circle can be used in protection, healing and conscious manifesting work. Request that the relevant angels attend the northern, southern, eastern and western quarters of the circle, with Sandalphon below and Metatron above. Ask the angels to return once the work is done and give thanks.

Bringers of Peace

Angels are not there to be idolised or worshipped in any way. Instead we give all the glory to God or to the divine source, whatever you wish to call it. Angels act on God's behalf by bringing peace to the world, and this may be one person at a time. It is their divine mission to help bring about a more peaceful world. If we live our life in a more peaceful way we are in tune with our authentic self. By connecting with the angels they can help us achieve this.

Your angels can help with all aspects of your life. Regularly ask your angels for help and guidance with situations, however large or small. However, angels cannot interfere with divine law. You cannot use them to exert your will over others. There are some experiences we must go through to learn. Learning is the point of our existence on the Earth plane. If they can help they will. If it is a life experience you must go through you can be safe in the knowledge that the angels are by your side, supporting you all the way.

If anyone you come into contact with is violent, aggressive or abusive, ask the angels to assist instead of reacting to them. Sometimes people react in a negative way through fear, pain or ignorance, so ask the angels to help protect you from such negativity.

Angel Altars

My angels guided me to the items needed for my altar, and they can do the same for you. Decide where you want to make a dedicated space. It can be in your bedroom or in any quiet space in your home. It can even be a space under the stairs. Ask the angels to guide you to make a space and find the items you need for your altar.

An angel altar can become a place for spiritual enlightenment, a place to connect to your angels and to gain insight into life. It can be a place where you let go of stresses and strains and put perspective into situations, revealing valuable insight. It can be a place of serenity, harmony, balance and, above all, a place where you can find peace.

The altar can be set up on a shelf or on top of a chest of drawers. Place the altar where you can see it and where you can spend time in quiet reflection. Have a comfy chair you can sit on. If the altar is in the bedroom you may just wish to use the bed as a seat. Decorate your altar with a beautiful cloth. I like to choose plain cloth in gold or white – something simple. Place a candle on your altar to light each time you spend time connecting and meditating. You can also use incense or aromatherapy oils in a burner to create beautiful aromas. Make sure any candles or incense burn safely, and never leave flames unattended.

Crystals, flowers, shells and feathers make pretty additions to your altar, as well as pictures and photos. Angel ornaments and angel images are easily bought and can be used on your altar. Make your altar as appealing as you can. This is your space to connect. When you have finished, dedicate your space to the angels and invite them in. Ask them to bless your altar and know that anytime you wish to connect with the angels you can spend time with them in your sacred space.

Angel Prayers

These prayers came to me during the summer of 2015. I have used them to great effect at various times. They are put here for personal use. I have included here prayers to the goddess Quan Yin.

Morning Prayer to St Michael

I give thanks for the day ahead,
And ask St Michael to protect me at all times,
To surround my being with a bubble of love and light,
So that I may shine,
And repel all negativity
That I may encounter
And to fill my day with happiness and joy,
So it is.
Thank you.

Prayer to Quan Yin

I ask Quan Yin and the angels of the violet flame
To colour my path with violet,
To protect me in my travels today,
So that everything goes well today
And every day,
According to divine order,
So it is.
Thank you.

Evening Prayer to the Angels

I give thanks for all I have experienced today,
For all the people I have encountered,
And I ask to let go of all troubles and worries,
So that I may sleep soundly
And be restful,
And wake up ready for the new day,
Full of positive intent,
So it is.
Thank you.

For Decluttering

I ask Archangel Michael and his legion of angel helpers,
To assist me in decluttering my mind and my home,
So that I may progress with ease and flow,
To have more energy and space,
In my physical and mental realms,
So that I may be at one

With my mind, home and well-being,
And able to invite positive energies and
experiences,
So it is.
Thank you.

For Healing

I ask Archangels Michael and Raphael
To assist in this powerful healing,
To remove all pain, fear and suffering,
To place (*name*) on the road to recovery,
To give courage, strength and peace,
And well-being,
For the highest good of all,
So it is.
Thank you.

Removing Negativity

I ask Quan Yin and the angels of the violet flame
To transmute all negative energies,
Surrounding (*name*),
Leaving only positive, peaceful and loving
experiences,
For the highest good of all,
So it is.
Thank you.

For Relationships

I ask Archangel Michael and his legions of light,
To transmute any negativity,
And restore my relationships,
With balance, harmony, peace and love,
So that I may be free from fear and harm,
And request that Archangel Michael
Uses his sword of truth,
To cut ties with all that no longer serves,
For my highest good,
So it is.
Thank you.

For Abundance

I ask Archangel Ariel and her fairy realm
To lavish me with abundance,
So that I may be free
To express myself fully,
In love and joy,
And have enough to share.
I give thanks for these wondrous gifts,
And know that it is for my highest good,
And for those around me,
So it is.
Thank you.

Angel Meditation – Connecting with the Angelic Realm

This is an initial meditation to connect with the angelic realm. The idea here is to move through the various energetic realms. This meditation moves our consciousness up to the higher planes.

If you wish you may begin by burning incense and/or lighting a candle (ensure that they are burning safely). Candles and incense are symbols of purification and enlightenment.

Make sure you will not be disturbed. Switch off the phone. Sit comfortably with your feet flat on the floor. If you're short, like me, you can put your feet on a cushion on the floor.

Begin by taking a few breaths, and breathe away all tension, stress and negativity. As you breathe, feel your body fill with peace, love and light as you take in each breath.

Know and feel that you are sitting in your chair. As you see yourself in your mind's eye, sitting in your chair, visualise the walls of the room that you are in falling away. There are no boundaries, only space. There are no limitations. Above you and around you is only space.

Now, begin to feel yourself, your spirit self, lift upwards. Feel your spirit self expand and move upwards. Feel yourself expand upwards, towards the sky. Feel yourself reaching out to the outer rim of the universe. As you feel yourself lifting, you feel yourself move into the spiritual realm, the world of spirit.

Spend a few moments here. You feel peaceful, relaxed and loved. You may see someone you know. Perhaps someone will speak to you. This is the realm of spirit. Notice how it feels. Feel that it is a peaceful place.

It is time to move higher throughout the realms. As you move higher and higher you feel lighter and lighter, more peaceful and of light.

Now you move upwards again. You are moving towards the realm of the ascended masters. You feel the peace and love of the ascended ones, who welcome you with joy and happiness. You explore this realm for a while. Perhaps one of the masters will bestow a gift on you or impart some wisdom.

Now, it is time to move on, even higher.

You move now towards the realm of the angelic. Feel your energy lift up out of the realm of the ascended ones towards that of the angels and the archangels. As you arrive in the angelic realm, you feel lighter, freer and more peaceful. It is a feeling of sheer bliss. You feel the loving, peaceful warmth of the angels. It is brighter here.

Perhaps an angel speaks to you or you hear angel music. Spend a while here and enjoy the loving, peaceful energies.

Next you are going to lift further, further than the angelic towards God, the divine source.

As you lift higher and higher you feel lighter and lighter. It gets brighter and brighter. You feel the unconditional love and feel fully at one with the *source of all creation. In this realm you will see nothing, but will experience the immense energy and the unconditional love and peace of the divine. Enjoy this energy for a while.*

You give thanks for your connection with the divine. You know that you can come back at any time. It is now time to begin the journey back towards the physical realm.

You begin to descend back into the angelic realm. You stay here for a few moments.

You give thanks for your time with the angels as you descend towards the realm of the ascended masters. You spend a few moments here.

You give thanks for your time with the masters and you descend now towards the realm of spirit.

You spend a few moments in the realm of spirit. You give thanks for your time here as you descend back into the physical realm, into your body, into the chair.

You see the walls of the room in your mind's eye materialising back to how it was when you first started.

As you begin to be more aware, you bring your awareness to the breath as you breathe in and out.

Now bring your attention to your fingers and toes. Wriggle them as you begin to become more aware of your body. Stretch and reach down to your toes, or as far as you can comfortably, and feel yourself becoming more grounded.

Open your eyes when you are ready. If you feel very spaced out, clap your hands and stamp your feet.

Finally, write down all that you have experienced into your journal.

This meditation has taken you through the various realms. There are many more realms to experience, but for now we have concentrated on these in particular. You will notice the change in energy as you pass through each realm. This meditation gives you the practice you need to move through to each one. One you have become more adept, you will be able to access each one with ease.

Each realm bears unique gifts that you can access: divine messages, healing and connection with the divine cosmos. Most of all you should feel and experience the love, peace and joy that these realms have to offer.

When we set about to create with a positive intent, with the help of the angels, something magical begins to happen. Opportunities will flow more easily, and wondrous synchronicities will begin to happen. Life will seem easier. You will be empowered and enriched as you surrender to the gift of the angels.

Task

When you first start inviting the angels into your life, begin each day by asking for a symbol or message. Don't be disappointed if you don't get a symbol or message straight away, as it may take time. When I first started working with the angels I would ask for and receive a symbol. When you receive a symbol, write it in a special journal then take time to let it 'speak' to you. If you can't relate to the symbol ask the angels to clarify its meaning. Many symbols and their meanings can be found on the Internet. Once you start working with symbols you will find them easier to interpret as you develop.

Use a positive affirmation each day with the assistance of the angels. Remember to keep it in the present and give thanks as if you already have what you have asked for.

Chapter 5

Working with Elementals and Nature Spirits

'All things bright and beautiful,
All creatures great and small,
All things wise and wonderful,
The Lord God made them all.'
Cecil Frances Alexander (1818-95)

It is said that the elementals exist on a plane somewhere between our own physical plane and the ethereal plane. They are not easily seen, and may appear as glimpses of light or movement just on the edge of your peripheral vision when out in nature. The elementals look after the elements of nature: earth, wind, fire and water. They are hence divided into four groups and they are the invisible, spiritual counterpart of visible nature. They are called gnomes, undines, sylphs and salamanders.

These names were given by Paracelsus, who taught that they were living entities, many resembling the human form. He believed that they could not be easily perceived because of the human race's underdeveloped senses.

According to Ted Andrews, in his book *How to Meet and Work with Spirit Guides* (1992), nature spirits have a hierarchical scheme:

Vowel	Element	Elemental Being	Overseeing Archangel
U	Earth	Gnomes	Uriel
O	Water	Undines	Gabriel
E	Air	Sylphs	Raphael
I	Fire	Salamanders	Michael
A	Ether		Christ

The Gnomes

The elementals that reside in the earth are the gnomes. It is said that there are as many types of gnomes as there are people. Their role is to look after the rocks, the crystals and minerals, and the flora and fauna of Mother Nature. Some gnomes look after the trees and the forests. It is believed that every shrub and tree has its own nature spirit.

When the gnomes work closely with humans and animals it is believed they work closest to the minerals of their own natures. Hence it is believed they have the ability to restore bones, which belong to the mineral kingdom.

Gnomes, like all elementals, should be treated with respect, as it is thought that they can be difficult and tricky to manage.

The Undines

The undines are the water elementals, and are restricted to their function within the element of water. They are often depicted as female, graceful and of beauty. They inhabit waterfalls, oceans, rivers, streams, marshes and literally anywhere where there is water.

Undines are believed to be human-like in appearance and of varying sizes, according to the water they look after. The undines work with the liquids and vital essences of human beings, plants and animals. They are considered emotional beings, and are often depicted riding dolphins and other fish.

The Sylphs

These beings reside in the element of air – not in the atmosphere as we experience it, but in the invisible, ethereal substance that is far more subtle. They were believed to live in the clouds, but their true home is on the tops of mountains. The ancients believed that they made snowflakes and clouds with the cooperation of the undines, who provided the moisture.

The sylphs are said to influence poets, artists and dreamers, inspiring them with the beauty of nature. The sylphs work with the gasses of animals and humans and, indirectly, with the nervous system.

The Salamanders

These beings reside in the spiritual ether, the invisible element of fire. Fire cannot exist without them, and mystics believed that they could be evoked by the ignition of fire. The ancients believed that by the burning of incense the presence of the salamanders would be felt.

Sometimes salamanders would appear as small balls of light. Some ancients believed that their appearance was that of lizard-like creatures.

Salamanders are considered the strongest and most powerful of the elementals. The salamanders work with humans and animals through body heat, the blood and the liver. Without them there would be no warmth.

Connecting

Try to connect with these spirits while out in nature. Early morning or evening are wonderful times for connecting with nature spirits. Just make sure that you are safe.

Sit somewhere quiet in nature. Quieten your mind and close your eyes. You may wish to hold a crystal or a special stone as you do this, which may attract the attention of the elementals. Imagine roots emanating from your feet, grounding you to the earth as you allow yourself to connect to the nature spirits. Notice any thoughts or feelings that come to you or changes in your energy field. When you have finished, give thanks for your experience and consciously disconnect.

The elementals may gift you stones and crystals, which might jump out at you while walking. Shells are also wonderful gifts of nature, as are feathers. Always give thanks for your gift and honour it. Treat gifts of stones and crystals as you would any crystal by cleansing them, and they can then be used for healing work and meditation. Learn to use them intuitively.

Treat nature spirits with respect, and honour them. Do not speak badly of fairies, or reveal their presence if you see one and it is meant to be secret. They will reveal themselves to those who need to see them at the time, and only when the time is right. Honour the nature spirits by respecting the environment. For me this includes recycling at home.

One can leave gifts of thanks to the nature spirits by leaving a little salt or tobacco for gifts that have been revealed to you. Fairies and elementals can help in earthly endeavours, particularly with material wealth. Sit quietly in nature, connect with the fairies and earth spirits and ask for their help. Leave your offering as thanks when you have finished. Archangel Uriel will also help you connect with the fairy and elemental kingdom, as she is the archangel of the Earth.

The elementals exist within the non-physical realm. They are not as highly vibrational as angels, but belong to a lower vibration outside the physical realm. The vibration of this realm is denser, but not as dense as our physical bodies. Paracelsus believed that the elementals could not be destroyed by the physical elements they looked after (for example, fire), but that they had a lifespan of between 300 and 1,000 years, at which point they did not die as humans do but resolved back into the primary essence from the essence they were associated with.

As with angels, each person's interpretation of what they see and experience differs. Practice and patience are key elements to experiencing the wonders of the elemental kingdom.

Task: Make a Fairy House

Honour your garden with ornaments of fairies and/or gnomes.

Make a fairy house at the bottom of your garden. There are lots of ideas for fairy houses online. You can make a house out of sticks, wood or anything you fancy, and adorn it with feathers, rocks, stones or shells. Make a little house for the little people in your garden or outdoor space. It can be as elaborate or as simple as you like.

- ❖ Andrews, Ted (1992) *How to Meet and Work with Spirit Guides*, Llewellyn Publications.
- ❖ Paracelsus (Philippus Aureolus Theophrastus Bombastus von Hohenheim) (1493-1541) was an alchemist and hermetic philosopher who wrote *De Occulta Philosophia*.

Chapter 6

Psychic Protection and Cleansing

Protecting and Strengthening the Aura from Negative Energies

'We are not human beings having a spiritual experience. We are spiritual beings having a human experience.'
Pierre Teilhard de Chardin

As we develop spiritually it is necessary that we protect the energy field that surrounds our bodies. This energy field is commonly known as the aura.

As we open up spiritually, we become like an open radio station, unable to control the volume and noise coming in from other sources. As we go about our daily business we encounter all kinds of negativity, anger and stress, which can deplete all the positive energies we have built up through our daily practice of meditation and mindfulness. Even our own thoughts can be negative. Protecting our energy field or aura is essential as we begin to be more and more sensitive to the energies we encounter during the day. There are many ways to cleanse the aura and protect it, and the techniques are quite simple.

Many times, when I was opening up spiritually, I found that I attracted people to me who were draining. You know the kind of people: the ones who are unhappy with their lives, miserable, full of negativity, and those who moan and complain. Stressful environments also take their toll. While one should remain non-judgemental when faced with these kinds of people – after all, we don't live their lives – it is vital to keep our energies uplifted and positive. Clearing (and protecting) our energy field is paramount, and helps to keep under control the negative debris we accumulate as we go about our day. Then can we begin to control our energies in a positive way. The more positive and enlightened we feel, the more positive experiences will come our way. Life will become more effortless as we begin to recognise when our energies are being depleted by negative external elements.

During the course of the day we encounter many things that drain our energy, including electrical fields that may be invisible, such as those from computers and mobile phones. In fact, any appliance that is connected to a mains electricity supply will give off electrical and magnetic fields when working. If we are mindful of this, we will notice the effects that working or passing through these electrical fields will have in our daily lives. So, at the end of the day make time to clear your energy field by meditation, even if it is only for a minute or so, and visualise your bubble of protection.

Taking a bath or shower at the end of the day and visualising the day's negative energies washing away is also a good way of strengthening your auric field and de-stressing. Cold showers, in particular, are excellent in strengthening the aura and ridding oneself of accumulated negative energy. I occasionally do this myself, and I must admit it takes some getting used to. You can try it by stepping into the shower just before the water gets warm. Cold water is excellent for the skin, as the cold contracts the underlying muscles. Walking outside on the earth without socks or shoes is another way to clear the aura, as it is grounding and is good for releasing negative energies.

As you progress on the spiritual path and therefore strengthen the auric field you will find that you move away from people or situations that no longer serve you. You will find yourself moving away from negative people and situations. You may find that your circle of friends changes as you seek out like-minded individuals who inspire you.

As you become more sensitive to the subtle energy shifts in your aura you will notice more and more how some people or situations drain your energy and how some people and situations uplift you. This will also be true of the things you watch on television. You may find yourself no longer watching the news or reading newspapers. You may also find yourself naturally turning to a more healthful, vegetable-based diet, or even turning totally vegan. All these things will influence your energies as you move away from things that deplete your energy. Many of these changes will be prompted from your higher guidance. As you become more spiritually aware these positive influences will become more and more prominent.

Smoking, alcohol, caffeine, illegal drugs and even chocolate have a depleting, negative influence on your aura. Fast foods, foods that have been genetically modified, the flesh from animals that have had no quality of life prior to being slaughtered and foods that are full of additives all have a negative effect on the aura… The list goes on.

Choosing a healthy, organic, vegetable-based diet and choosing clean living are the keys to living positively and energetically. There is a lot of literature out there to help you on your way, and there are many support groups that will assist you in changing your lifestyle and helping combat addictions. You can also ask the angels to help, or your guardian angel, guides, God, Jesus or any other enlightened being to assist. *Ask and it shall be given; seek and you will find* is a passage in the Bible that I use time and again, and it is true. Put the thought out there into the universe for help and guidance to make positive changes in your lifestyle. All you need to do is believe and it will appear.

Cleansing Bath

Having a bath with a handful of rock salt is good for restoring balance to the auric field. As you bathe, visualise the debris of the day melting away. Aromatherapy oils can also be added, which will also relax the senses and de-stress. Make the experience a spiritual one, as the bath will get rid of physical and also your spiritual dirt.

Epsom salts (hydrated magnesium sulphate) are also a good addition to a hot bath as they act to cleanse the aura, to detoxify and to de-stress, plus a whole host of other benefits. Add two cups to hot water.

For those of you who don't like taking baths, take a shower instead and visualise the spray of the water cleansing away all negativity. Using the power of positive intent, as with all things spiritual, can be just as effective. If you are a reiki practitioner you can put your symbols into the shower head, and visualise the symbols cleansing your aura as you shower.

My reiki teacher recommended a cold shower as being very good for cleansing the aura. Cold showers give a whole host of other physical effects, including improved circulation, and leave you feeling invigorated. Start with cold water and gradually increase the temperature.

Drawing Down the White Light

The white light meditation (found in Chapter 1) is excellent at cleansing the aura, and the white light can be used at any time to cleanse away negativity in an instant. If you are in a stressful environment or are unable to focus, take some time out, even if the only quiet space you can find is in the loo. Take a few deep breaths and connect with the source. Visualise the white light and draw it down through the top of the head as you breathe in. Take a few breaths, breathing in the white light until you feel harmonised. Visualise it taking away any negativity and energetic debris as it leaves you feeling calm and centred. The more you do this simple exercise the quicker you will be able to do it at any time and feel its effects.

Cord Cutting with Archangel Michael

Each of us is connected by etheric cords of light that can develop as we progress through life. These cords develop as we develop relationships with others. These can be friendships, as couples, business relationships, acquaintances and so on. Some ethereal cords are permanent, such as cords of attachment with our children, which should never be cut. We can develop these etheric connections with every person we come into contact with. Some of these connections can be pleasant, some not so. Cord cutting can be a useful tool in cutting etheric cords with those who drain us energetically, those who have upset us, or those who we have fear- or anger-based relationships with.

Cord cutting is a wonderful exercise and I have come across a number of variations, but I like to envision Archangel Michael overseeing this as he ensures that the cord cutting is done in a loving way and without harm or hate. By cord cutting you are not harming the other person. You are removing fear-based emotions. As people pop into our thoughts and interactions, etheric cords develop between us and the other person. When disharmony develops between people, cord cutting can be a useful tool, particularly if you are projecting negative thoughts or feelings towards one another.

This etheric cord cutting exercise is done using Archangel Michael and his sword of truth as he severs cords that no longer serve us. In doing this visualisation other cords that you are unaware of can also be severed. Having Archangel Michael by your side during this exercise will ensure that all cord cutting is completed in a loving way.

Sit in a quiet place where you will not be disturbed. You can light a candle and incense if you wish. Ask Archangel Michael to assist you in your cord cutting. You may have a person in mind who you may feel you need to cut cords with – for example, an ex-partner. See the cord between you and the other person, and ask Archangel Michael to assist you in cutting this and any other etheric cords as needed. Visualise Archangel Michael removing the cords from your body. You may even see cords attached to you in unusual places such as your feet, your arms or your torso. Now visualise a bowl, a cauldron or any other vessel that contains a pure light. See the cords that have been severed placed into this vessel of light to be cleansed and transmuted. Now ask Archangel Michael to heal the areas from where the cords have been removed so that you and the other person are whole. Envision yourself healed, full of light and free from unwanted etheric cords. Finish the exercise by taking a few breaths and seal and protect the aura above the head, below the feet and side to side at arm's length all around in love, light and peace.

Asking the Angels for Protection

If you feel under attack, unsettled or vulnerable, you can use the power of positive intent and ask the angels to assist you and give you protection. They can also be asked to protect your home, your car, your place of work or any other place that you feel needs it. You are not taking them away from other service work, as they are omnipresent. Ask and the protection will be there.

When protecting your home you can ask an angel to guard the house on all four corners or ask an angel to protect the front and back entrances. You can even ask the angels to protect your tent if you're out camping.

Be mindful to send any negativity away with peace and light.

If you have spirits around you that are draining you can ask the angels to guide them on their way back to the light. As you develop spiritually you will find that spirits will be attracted to your light energy.

As I was developing spiritually I experienced regular physical phenomena happening in the house. Doorbells would ring when there was no one there. This would often happen as family members were pulling on to the drive or walking outside the house. It was as if the spirits were letting me know that they were there and it was not some knock-a-door-and-run-away game that a child would play to irritate the neighbours. The TV would switch on in the middle of the night, the microwave would beep randomly, and at one point the kettle would switch itself on. I asked the spirits out loud not to do certain things, particularly with regard to the kettle. I asked the angels to assist in leading any spirits who were lost back to the light. I thanked them for their presence and asked the angels to see them on their way. The activity, which was never frightening in any way, eased off. Every now and then the spirits come back to visit, and ring the doorbell or switch on the TV in the middle of the night. Somehow I feel it comforting to know that they are around every now and again.

Cleansing the Home

Cleansing the home with sage (smudging) is a good way to clear negative debris that may build up over time. Burning of herbs and oils in ritual cleansing is common to many cultures, and can be found in shamanic practices and in churches alike. Smudging the home or yourself or another person is like having an energetic shower. It will get rid of negativity. Crystals or other objects can be cleansed by passing them through sage smoke to clear away negative debris.

Arguments, negative behaviour, violent games or films bring with them negative vibes. These can be cleared away through positive intent and the burning of sage. The environment will be immediately uplifted once the sage is lit and the smoke drifts into the environment. Set the positive intention of cleansing away negative debris before lighting your sage.

Bundles of sage can be bought online or from most New Age stores. There are various combinations of sage and other dried herbs for smudging. Use your intuition to know what feels right. I personally prefer white sage smudging sticks.

Before lighting the sage stick set your intention. Light one end and blow on it a little to get the smoke going. Place it on a heatproof dish or on an abalone shell. Direct the smoke with your hand or a feather wand or fan. If smudging a room, walk around the perimeter, paying special attention to the corners, and ask for all negativity to be cleansed or say a small prayer. Do it with reverence and love, and when the cleansing is done give thanks for the positive energy that has been imbued into your home.

If you are a reiki practitioner, you can use your reiki symbols as well.

Using Visualisation as Space Clearing

Another way to clear the home energetically, if you have no sage, is by visualisation. It may be slow to start, but as you practise this method and become more adept it will get easier. Visualisation, like anything else, is an acquired skill, and some people find it easier than others.

If an area in the home has a dense energy and has never been cleared before, It can take a little while to the clear the area.

Start by sitting in a quiet space where you will not

be disturbed. Take a few breaths to quieten your mind. Ask the angels to assist you in your work and request the angels associated with the violet ray, who will transmute any negative energies.

Visualise the room you are in being filled with the colour violet. It may appear as violet smoke. See this violet smoke build up and fill every corner and crevice of the room, removing all negativity and replacing it with positive, peaceful, loving energy. Now extend the violet smoke into other rooms of the house, including the attic, cellar, utility room, garage, shed and such, if you have these. Know that you are transmuting all negative energy as it travels along, restoring balance and harmony in the home.

When you have done give thanks to the angels and unseen helpers who have assisted you in your work.

This exercise can also be done in a car (but not while driving), the workplace or any other place where you feel it is needed.

Colouring Your Path

This technique can also be used to colour your path.

If you have an important meeting to go to or just want to set a positive path for your day ahead as well as give you protection from negative influences, ask the angels of the violet ray to colour your path violet.

Sit in quiet meditation. Take a few deep breaths and visualise the day ahead and the tasks that need to be completed. Imagine that a there is a road or path set before you. This road or path can appear how you like it (mine is always one straight road in front of me). Visualise the violet energy and the angels of the violet flame coming through and placing the violet colour on your path ahead. You could visualise, instead of a path, a room or the place you are going to if you are familiar with it.

I have successfully used this technique time and time again, especially at work, when I know that I am going to encounter stressful situations, or when I am travelling to new places for interviews and so on. It has helped calm my nerves and has dispelled any threatening atmospheres. I also use it on my travels so that I may have a safe and stress-free journey. You can use this technique as part of your daily practice.

Letting Go of Fear

If we see ourselves as stuck – with our finances, our relationships or our jobs, etc. – we need to move out of the victim mindset. We need to let go of the worry and have a deep knowing that what will be, will be. It is about letting go and surrendering to the life flow force. If we spend our time worrying it is time wasted. We need to be in the now, in the present. There is no point worrying about the future and there is no point worrying about what is past.

To be mindful of the present moment releases us from the constraints of our victim mindset. Once we become mindful of this we are able to release our minds and our lives to the moment and to surrender all fear-based thoughts of worry. We often worry about things that in actual fact we may have no control over. This does not mean that we should go out and be reckless, recklessly spending all our money and leaving nothing for food. This means to be mindful of the present and of our need to survive, to nourish our bodies in the present moment and to look after our families. We need to know that if we let go of fear and surrender to the moment that nothing can harm us. Only our own fear-based thoughts can do that.

We need to let go of our fears, as the fear-based mindset is that of the ego. It is not part of our spiritual selves. You may be thinking that this is easier said than done. Indeed, it is easy to slip into fear when our lives are so hectic. How are we to pay the mortgage each month? How can we deal with the behaviour of others that drags us down each day? How do we cope with the commute to work? How do I deal with the unhappy relationship that I am in? We may think that many of these things are out of our control, and indeed they may be. But to tackle these issues we must first change our mindset from one of fear to one of loving. We need to know that the universe will provide for us, and we need to surrender our fears to the divine. We can ask for assistance in releasing our fears and therefore changing our lives for the better.

One example of this was when I started to do my degree as an undergraduate. The first year was so difficult. I was a mature student with two young children, and I hated every moment of it. During the summer I felt dread at going back and yet I knew that I wanted to do it. So, I changed my thinking and decided that I was going to go back and *enjoy* it. I went back after the summer and, although it was hard work, I can say I did enjoy it and completed it with ease. Simply changing our mindset can alter many things, and can turn our thoughts from those of negativity and fear to those of positivity and love. In this way we begin to be more in tune with our spiritual self and we find ourselves in synchronicity with life rather than feeling out of step and out of control.

We can surrender our fears to the divine, to the angels of light, to our spiritual guides and masters. In turn they will guide us, but we need to sit and listen. Meditation can play a great part in helping us open our ears to the divine and to the messages of the angels, guides and masters. Through calming our bodies and minds with meditation our fears and anxieties may not appear so great, and may even disappear altogether. Eventually we may notice that we are on a synchronistic path where events, circumstances and happenings will happen at the right time, as if by magic. We will realise that even the challenges we face from day to day happen for a reason.

What should we do when we face challenges in our daily life? Being spiritual does not mean being a doormat, and we should be able to stand up for what we believe in. However, we should stand up for our beliefs and values in a loving way, by being assertive but never aggressive. Sometimes when someone is angry they will try to goad people into verbal or physical conflict, as if they were justifying their anger. By acknowledging this and by not getting drawn into anger ourselves, but by being assertive, we can overcome conflict.

Whenever I come into contact with negative people I visualise myself in a pink bubble that protects me from their negativity. Afterwards, I align myself by thinking about what matters to me the most and what brings me love, such as my children, my husband and my family. Another example of this is a trick a colleague taught me. We were working in a difficult environment with young people who had challenging behaviour. If things descended into chaos during the session, my friend would transport herself off on a journey to a favourite place she had visited. That way, even if only for a few moments, she could come away from the drama and put herself into a happy place.

Simply by changing our thoughts we can change our world. Thoughts and feelings are very powerful: they can make our lives better or worse in an instant. By letting go and surrendering to the divine, by letting go of fear and by being more positive, loving and peaceful, we can empower ourselves and create a life which we deserve: one of happiness, well-being and contentment.

Task: The Auric Bubble Breath

This breathing exercise can be used to strengthen and purify the body's energetic field. I use this after meditating to seal and protect my aura.

Sit comfortably, with the feet flat on the floor. Breathe in and visualise the breath up travelling up from your feet, up the rear of your body, up and over your head. On the out breath visualise the breath travelling down over the front of your body towards the feet. In all do this five times in a circular motion, each time visualising the breath moving further away from the body into the auric field. Next, breathe in and visualise the breath travelling from the feet up the left side of the body towards the top of the head. On the out breath visualise the breath travelling down the right side of the body down towards the feet. Again, do this circular breathing motion five times in total, visualising each time the breath moving away from the body further into the auric field.

This breathing action will cleanse and strengthen the aura, while letting go of tension and stress. You can do this morning or evening and after any meditation practice.

You can visualise an imaginary bubble of protection around your aura, which protects it. This bubble should be transparent, translucent. If the bubble surrounding your energy field is visualised to be too solid in form, you may find yourself isolated from others during the day. This may seem unbelievable.

If so, try it. Do what makes you feel best and make notes on how you feel.

If you surround yourself in a bubble and opportunities seem not to come your way, open the bubble up slightly at the front to allow more opportunities to manifest. This would be applicable especially if you wanted to attract clients into your life.

The bubble of protection should help deflect negativity during the course of the day. If you find yourself in a particularly stressful situation you can visualise yourself in a pink bubble of light for added protection. If during the day you are feeling stressed, take time in the bathroom to realign yourself by taking a few deep breaths and visualising your bubble of protection. To realign your energies all that needs to be done is to think of someone that brings a sense of love. Who do you love the most? What makes you happy? Focus on the important things in life and this should help alleviate the stress.

Chapter 7

Spiritual Healing

'All healing is first a healing of the heart.'
Carl Townsend

Many of today's illnesses can be attributed to the strains and stresses of modern-day living. To a greater or lesser extent many illnesses are psychosomatic. Although the physical symptoms of the illness may be treated, the underlying cause will still be there and the illnesses may resurface again, perhaps in a different form.

Everything is made up of vibrating energy particles, including our bodies. The purpose of spiritual healing is to align ourselves as a healer to God, the divine, in our true light, and to help bring into alignment the client who we are working with.

We live in a material, physical world, and we get through our day as best we can. We 'forget' about our spirit and our divine path as we stumble through our day-to-day existence. Unfortunately, many people reconnect with their spiritual self only when disaster strikes, by way of a major life change such as the death of a loved one, divorce or a life-threatening health condition such as cancer.

It is at this point that we may question the purpose of life and reconnect with the divine. People affected in these ways may realise that the ego has ruled their life. They have been chasing after a bigger house, a better car and more money. At the point of a life-changing event it suddenly becomes meaningless and empty. We turn to other sources for answers to our questions. Why has this happened to me? As healers we connect to the divine source, and in turn we hopefully help others to reconnect and tune back in.

The body is an energy system made up of atoms that vibrate. The brain itself works through a series of electrical impulses that can be scientifically measured.

The body is surrounded by what is known as the aura, which is likened to an energetic field that surrounds the body. The four fields or subtle bodies of the aura are the physical, the emotional or astral, the mental and the spiritual. These fields expand outwards from the body. The chakra system (see the chapter on chakras) helps link through the aura and into these fields. Any imbalances in any of these fields can manifest into the physical. Just think of how stress can impact on one's physical well-being. Research is discovering more and more how stress can develop into physical symptoms.

Over time the chakras can become imbalanced, and this can manifest in the physical body. Such imbalances can appear as problems, not just in the physical but also the emotional, mental and spiritual fields. Hands-on healing helps to restore balance to the aura and to the chakra system.

Vibrational healing can assist in the balancing of the chakra system and the subtle bodies. Unfortunately for some people who have certain belief systems, vibrational healing, especially that which is done through the laying on of hands, can be quite a challenging thought. Vibrational healing, however, is complementary to more contemporary methods. Vibrational healing can help to restore one's natural flow of energy within the body.

Hands-on healing is as old as time itself. It is still practised within many faiths. To my mind, the greatest healer who ever lived was Jesus.

Divine Guidance

Deceased loved ones and some spirit guides flit between the spirit world and the physical world to give messages and hope to those on the physical plane. Angels, ascended masters and evolved spiritual guides help us to realign to God's divine plan and to live our lives in the best possible spiritual truth. When we connect with our soul's purpose, the worries, stresses and strains fade away. The physical realm no longer enslaves us and we are free to be whom we wish. We live our life in the light and in peace and harmony.

When working with clients we listen to our own intuition and divine guidance but also give the client the opportunity to tune in and listen to their divine guidance, and to tune in to their authentic self.

Blocks to Healing

To be able to heal others we must see that our client is an expression of divine perfection. Their spiritual self is perfect in every way and part of God's divine plan. We, as healers, must set aside our own ego and any judgement. The person in front of us should be viewed as perfect in every way, and it is our role to remind them of this and to help them begin the process of loving themselves as God loves them.

We, as healers, should open our hearts to God's love and act as a channel and help our client to connect to that love. We act as a conduit for God's divine love, which we then channel and impart through our hands, hearts and minds. One should see through the client's ego and feel no sorrow or pity, but empathise with them. Clients should be allowed room for self-expression, which may be released in the form of anger, pain or sorrow. Don't feed the emotions as they develop, but remain detached yet loving. Give your client room to release their fears and anxieties in a loving and controlled way. A powerful healing can release powerful emotions, and once this release has happened it can allow the client to move on, spiritually and emotionally.

Conducting a Healing Session

Make sure you have a chat to your client. This helps them to relax, and also gives you the opportunity to explain what the healing session entails. It also gives the client the opportunity to tell you what is troubling them and to indicate any causes. It is important to be relaxed in order to attune to the healing energies.

To act as a channel for these healing energies one should be fully relaxed and open and be willing to act as a clear conduit. Remember you are acting as a channel; you are not giving your own energy. Always explain to the client what is to happen if they are new to you. Make them as comfortable and relaxed as possible. The healing session is in no way a substitute for medical intervention, but is complementary to it. Do not promise any cures or advise on medication. You are not a doctor.

When you are ready to start the healing session, visualise your energy field expanding upwards, connecting to the divine source and healing guides and angels. Feel your energy and that of your healing guides and angels merge as one. Ask that your guides and angels are of 100 per cent light, and don't be afraid to ask for the highest evolved beings that you can access. By doing this you are ensuring that you are not pulling towards you any lower energies that may be attracted by your light and the work you are about to do. Some spirit entities are like people – nosy – and want to see what's going on.

Start to focus on your feet, which are rooting you to the ground. Raise both hands in the air. I like to think of this as being a satellite dish to channel as much of the energy as possible. You may feel the energy coming in. I tend to feel it as a slight rocking motion backwards and forwards throughout my body.

When you feel attuned, keep your right hand uplifted and lower your left hand. Ask for all negativity to be released from you through your left hand. Imagine a bucket or bowl of light on the floor capturing all the negative elements, transmuting them back to light. Ask that you are a pure conduit for the healing that is about to take place. Now raise your left hand in the air again and ask for permission to heal your client. You may wish to say your client's name at this point.

Your focus during the healing session should be one of love, peace and divine radiance.

The Act of Healing

Your client may be seated or may be lying comfortably on a therapy bed. If they are seated make sure their feet are connected to the ground. If their legs are short, place a cushion under their feet.

As a rule of thumb, do not touch the body between the nipples and the knees, as in this way you keep yourself and the client safe and relaxed. Healing energies can be beamed into certain areas without the need for touch.

Begin the healing session by gently touching the client's shoulders. Raise your hands to the crown of the client's head. Be aware of the energy flowing from her and of the energy flowing through your hands. Scan the energy centre of the chakras at around six inches from the body and beam the healing energies through your hands, which act as a conduit and channel the healing.

From the crown chakra, scan and send healing to:

❖ The brow
❖ The throat
❖ The heart
❖ The solar plexus
❖ The abdomen
❖ The base of the spine.

Note any areas that feel 'different'. You may feel hot, cold or prickly sensations. This can be an indication of the chakra being out of balance.

For seated clients scan the front and the back of the chakra. For prone clients just scan the front.

You can then scan and channel healing energy into the body's natural energy field, starting at the head.

Then scan down the body from the nape of the neck down the spine.

Return to the right shoulder. Scan from the shoulder down the arm to the fingertips.

Scan the base of the spine to the hip.

Then scan from the hip to the knee.

Scan from the knee down to the foot.

Repeat for the left side.

When you have completed the scan place both hands lightly on the feet. The client, especially if seated, may feel a drawing down sensation. This ensures that the client is grounded at the end of the session. For the seated client, place both hands firmly over the top of the feet. For the prone client, hold both feet in your hands or place your palms on the bottom of the feet.

At this point you may quickly scan the chakras and revisit any areas that still feel out of balance. Use your intuition.

Concluding the Healing

Return the hands to the shoulders of your client and give thanks to your client and the guides or angels for the healing session.

Withdraw from your client and realign yourself. You may brush yourself down with the hands to completely disconnect and remove any spiritual debris. You may wish to go through some deep breathing with the client to bring them back to full awareness. Rouse your client gently, and offer some water. Ensure that the client is fully aware and sufficiently grounded for when they leave.

Listen to what your client has to say about the session and respond appropriately in a positive manner. You may wish to record their responses for future sessions. You can give your client feedback on your feelings or sensations that arose during the session. All comments should be kept positive and constructive.

A Note on Professionalism

You may have found it in your heart that you wish to heal and give to others who are in need. In today's society there is a great need for healing services. The healing routine that has been given in the previous section is guidance on how to give a healing. However, if you wish to take it further and act as a professional healer, you will find that there are many organisations with which you can take a course and register as a professional. Here are some ways with which you can take a certified programme in the United Kingdom.

- ❖ Reiki (various)
- ❖ The Spiritualists' National Union
- ❖ The Healing Trust
- ❖ The Harry Edwards Healing College
- ❖ The Healer Practitioner Association International.

These are but a few. There are many reiki master teachers out there, and many varying forms of reiki. Try to find a reliable teacher of reiki through recommendation and/or reputation.

Preparation for Healing

- ❖ Self – Ensure personal cleanliness, particularly the breath and hands. I like to use a few drops of juniper essential oil on my hands.
- ❖ Environment – Ensure the room is clean and airy. Select calming, meditative background music that has no words. I like to cleanse any room I use, before and after, using a sage smudge stick. You can dedicate the room as a healing space by whatever means you wish. Intention is all.
- ❖ Starting – Ensure the individual is comfortable and aware of what the healing routine entails.

Breathe them into a state of relaxation or use a visualisation to begin.

If you decide to heal professionally, the keeping of records and confidentiality is an important factor. As part of your professional training you should be taught how to keep accurate records and be made aware of any legislation that may be in place, such as the Data Protection Act (UK). Professional insurance is a must to protect not only yourself but others as well.

Distant Healing and the Power of Prayer

Distant healing is also an effective way of sending out healing. Again, it is all down to intent. If you believe it will work, it invariably will. I have had many successes with sending out distant healing. I send out distant healing during my morning meditations to those who need it.

It is better that you have the consent of the person who you are sending it to. If you don't you can request for the healing to be accepted, or if it is not, that the healing is transmuted into the universe for the benefit of others who will accept it.

Begin by going into a meditative state with a few slow, deep breaths. Draw your attention to calling in your guides and healing angels for this healing work. Ask permission to give this healing to the person. Imagine the healing energies coming through your hands. You can beam the energy to the other person through your hands. This is a method that beams the healing energy over distance to the recipient. I like to think that my hands act like satellite dishes beaming the energies. You can focus on a particular part of the recipient's body or you can just send healing energies to wherever the recipient needs it. When you feel you have finished, give thanks for the healing and disconnect from that person. This can be done by sweeping your hand down the front of your body to disconnect, or imagine that you are pushing the recipient away with the sweeping of your hand.

More focused absent healing can also be completed by using a teddy or a doll as a substitute. Simply lay your hands on the teddy as if giving healing to a person and imagine the healing energies being transferred to the recipient. Again, at the end of the session, ensure that you disconnect from the recipient. Make note of any feelings, emotions or physical things you that come to you.

It is important that you treat any client with the utmost respect and do not divulge personal information to anyone. Confidentiality is important, as it not only protects the client but also establishes trust between the client and the healer.

Chapter 8

Conscious Manifesting with the Moon

'Everyone is a moon, and has a dark side which he never shows to anybody.'
Mark Twain

The moon is a beautiful, enchanting and mysterious sight in the night sky. The moon holds such power and is intrinsically connected with the push and pull of the Earth because it regulates the rolling tides. Working with the power of the moon can help tap into creative cycles. Being linked to the element of water, the moon is associated with emotions. Observing the phases of the moon is one way to be in tune with nature and the cycles of the Earth. Working with and tuning into each moon phase can help to delve deeper into creating our desires and assist in letting go of that which no longer serves.

It takes twenty-eight days for the moon to fully orbit the Earth. During this time it goes through four main stages, which are the new moon, the waxing moon, the full moon and the waning moon.

When we work with the moon cycle we gain intuition

and insight on the hidden elements of our spiritual self. We can work on manifesting and banishing that which no longer serves us at any time, but doing this while drawing on the power of the moon gives more energy and emphasis to our efforts.

The moon represents the goddess aspect. The sun represents the God aspect. Together they work in harmony and unison: the yin and yang of life.

The phases of the moon may affect our emotions. For example, if you are feeling low, unable to concentrate, or perhaps unexpectedly energetic, look at what the moon phase is. By looking at the cycles of the moon in this way we get in tune with our bodily cycles and make ourselves aware of why we may feel the way we do. Just as the lack of sun may make us feel down and flat, a sunny afternoon can energise and revitalise our energies. The moon cycle also may affect our emotions in more subtle ways and may affect us in many ways that we aren't even aware of.

The triple goddess is associated with the moon and she is symbolised by three female figures: maiden, mother and crone. These figures symbolise the three phases in a woman's life. The maiden possesses youthfulness, purity and newness, and symbolises the waxing phase of the moon. The mother is fertile and full of power, and symbolises the full moon. The crone is the old woman. She is full of wisdom and knowledge, and symbolises the waning phase of the moon. The male representation of the triple goddess is youth, warrior and sage.

Working with the energy of the moon isn't restricted

to women but is open to everyone. It is all part of what one can call conscious manifesting.

The waxing moon brings things to us, and is a time of manifesting. It is the time when the moon is developing from the new moon towards the full moon. It's a good time to start attracting things to us, so if you are looking for a new job now is the time to arrange an interview. The moon is progressing to complete fullness, so this is the time to use the moon's energy to fuel your actions.

The waning moon sends things away. It is a time of banishing and breaking old patterns that no longer serve us. It is a good time to declutter, to get rid of what no longer serves and to throw out rubbish. One can also banish bad habits or emotions that prevent us from moving forwards.

The period known as the dark moon is generally the phase a day or so prior to the new moon. This is when the waning moon has disappeared from the night sky before the new moon is visible. This is not the time to work with the power of the moon, but a time of rest and reflection. It is a time of meditating, of connecting to the divine source and of heightening psychic energies. It is also a good time to let go of personal grief or loss, which in itself can be quite liberating.

The moon's cycles are generally indicated on calendars. Or you can use an almanac, the Internet or even an app on your phone or tablet.

The New Moon

The new moon is when the moon is no longer visible from the Earth. The day after, a sliver of the moon can be seen, and it is at the point that the moon is entering its waxing phase. It is considered to be a new moon up to three and a half days after the actual day of the new moon.

During this moon phase it is a good time to start new projects. It is an excellent time to create vision boards, set new goals and plan new ventures. It is also a good time to get rid of old habits and behaviours by starting new ones. The new moon phase is a good time for attracting positive things, changing things, decluttering and for general good luck.

The new moon is a good time for manifesting. This is a good time for starting new projects, planning ahead and setting goals. It is also a good time for starting positive affirmations.

A Simple New Moon Ritual

Take some time to do this in your sacred space, where you will not be disturbed. Light a candle and/or some incense. You may wish to clear your space with sage beforehand. Sit comfortably and breathe slowly while you consciously connect to your higher self. Imagine roots coming from the soles of your feet, penetrating into the earth and grounding you. Take time to think about projects you may wish to start. Perhaps you want to start looking for a new job, starting that diet plan or a savings plan, doing projects around the home or maybe writing that book. Write it down on a sheet of paper. Always finish by writing, 'This, or something better, and for the highest good of all, so it harms none.' You can put this list on an altar, under a crystal or in a God box (a special box into which you put wishes or problems and turn them over to God to answer your prayers). Review your list, and at the next new moon edit it or make a new list.

You can make a vision board at this time as well. Cut out and stick or pin the things you wish to create in life on to a corkboard or on a large piece of paper or card. Or, if you're artistic, you can draw how you wish your life to be and things you want. Be creative and imaginative. You can then place your creation where you can see it or look at it regularly.

The Full Moon

The full moon can affect behaviour, concentration and mood. In my working environment I (and some of my colleagues) noticed how the full moon would affect the behaviour of young people, particularly adolescent males. It was on subtle levels, such as poor behaviour, giddiness and poor concentration. When I was completing my first degree, I noticed that I couldn't write assignments or do research on a full moon, as my concentration seemed poor.

When the moon is at its fullest, it shines its light on aspects of life that are no longer required. When you harvest the energy of the full moon you can make steps to manifest into your life what you desire, and by doing so eliminate that which no longer serves you.

When the moon is full we need to take time to reflect. This is a good time to pay special attention to dreams and to creative endeavours. Revisiting goals and creative projects made on the new moon is also good at this time.

The full moon is the moon of the mother, fertile and complete. Working in this phase can bring powerful results. Crystals can be left out under the light of the full moon to clear them energetically and to absorb the moonlight.

A Simple Full Moon Ritual

This is a wonderful exercise to do, and one which I do often on a full moon. It's a ritual of releasing and letting go in readiness to invite new energies in.

Go into your quiet space. This space can be cleansed energetically by visualising it as cleansed of negative energies or by burning sage. The choice is yours. You may like to dress a candle and light it. Small votive or spell candles are good for this exercise, as the candle will be allowed to burn itself out afterwards. You may also like to light some incense and have some favourite crystals nearby. Have a pen, some paper and a flameproof dish at hand.

Write on the piece of paper what you wish to release, what you wish to let go of physically and emotionally, and which limiting beliefs no longer serve you. Take your time to reflect. When you have finished, you can write, 'For the highest good of all. It is so.'

Take your paper and light one corner. When it is burning, place it in the flameproof dish. Take care not to burn yourself or your surroundings. Visualise your intentions being released into the universe to be transmuted. The ashes can be thrown into the earth, into flowing water or into the air, to be swept away afterwards.

Sit quietly in meditation to see if anything else arises. You may wish to write anything that crops up, or about how you feel in your journal. This will be good to reflect on at a later date. Allow your candle to burn down.

Task: The Full Moon Meditation

This meditation may be done at any phase of the moon, but will have more meaning if done on the night of the full moon.

Light a white candle, burn incense if you wish, and sit in your quiet space where you will not be disturbed. You may wish to play soft meditation music in the background. This is your time, a time for peace and clarity.

Start by closing your eyes and taking a few deep breaths. As you inhale, breathe in the white light of the divine consciousness and peace. As you breathe out, visualise all your worries and stresses leaving your body as if they are some grey smoke. Feel all your troubles melt away. Continue in this way for a few breaths.

Now begin to concentrate on your feet. See roots as if they are roots of a tree sprouting from the soles of your feet, connecting you to the ground as they travel down into the earth and grounding you.

It is night-time. You are outdoors, and you find yourself standing in front of a large oak gate set in a high stone wall. You cannot see what is beyond the gate or the wall. You reach for the latch on this gate and push it open. As you step through the oak gate you see there is a path ahead. You close the gate behind you as you step on to the path.

You look up to the night-time sky and see it is clear and filled with multitudes of stars twinkling in the heavens. The moon is full and bright and it illuminates the path ahead. You see that there is grass either side of the path.

The path leads to a lake, lit by the moonlight shimmering on the still, dark waters. The night is quiet, still and illuminated by the glow of the moon. In the distance, you hear the faint call of an owl, but you are not frightened as you feel at ease and peaceful. You take a moment to look at your surroundings. Take a few moments to pause.

You now begin to walk the path towards the lake, and are captivated by the moonlight shimmering on the reflective surface of the water. You notice that by the side of the lake there is a bench where you can sit down and look upon the water. The bench is underneath an oak tree. Its branches stretch out to give a protective canopy of leaves. You hear the leaves rustle slightly as the warm, gentle breeze moves through the outstretched branches.

You sit on the bench under the oak tree and gaze upon the water and the light of the full moon reflected upon it. As you look upon the lake images appear to you on the surface. The lake and the moon reflected on its surface reveal to you what changes you need to make in your life, and give you inspiration. You take a few moments to gaze across the water as the lake reveals its secrets to you. Take a few moments to pause.

When you are done you give thanks to the lake and the moon for revealing to you its insights. You reach into your pocket and find in it the flower petals. You take the petals out of your pocket and look at them. You walk to the edge of the lake with the petals in your hand and gently drop the petals in the lake as an offering of thanks. You take one last look at the lake and turn back towards the bench and the oak tree. You step once again on to the path and walk back to the oak gate set in the high stone wall. You open the oak gate and step through it, shutting the gate behind you.

You find yourself back, sitting in your quiet place. You begin to become aware of your body once more and the room you are sitting in. Wriggle your toes and fingers as you breathe in, and become aware of your surroundings. Open your eyes when you are ready. Run your hands down your legs towards your feet to truly ground yourself.

When you are ready, get your journal and pen and write down everything you can remember.

Chapter 9

Spiritual Candles

*'Look how a single candle can both defy
and define the darkness.'*
Anne Frank

Candles, which can be used for conscious manifesting and for setting positive intentions, are wonderful tools to work with. Candles have been used in ceremonies for millennia. Go into any church and you will find candles. They represent the flame of enlightenment and purity. Candles in the Christian Church represent Jesus's light as it shines on the world.

One of the simplest types of magical working and conscious manifesting is through candle burning. It is a simple form of ritual.

I love working with candles, and in the past I have made my own. There is nothing more satisfying than burning a home-made candle. Burning a home-made candle in meditation and manifesting can add more power to your workings.

Candles are available everywhere, especially in good New Age stores, where they can be purchased in a variety of colours. A plain dinner candle can be used, or a smaller votive candle. For the purposes of magical manifesting it is better to use dinner or smaller candles rather than large candles that take forever to burn down. The candle used to work with should be virgin (in other words, unused).

If you make your own candles you put your own personal vibration into the candle and attune the candle to the purpose of its intent. You can also add essential oils to the candle as you make it to add an aroma when burning. Candle making kits can be acquired from specialist stores, such as hobby and craft shops, or online.

Lighting a candle as part of your meditation practice sets the intent to connect with spirit, gives subtle lighting in the practical sense and incorporates one of the four elements into your practice, which is the element of fire.

The Four Elements

The notion of the four elements comes from the ancient Greeks, in that everything was made up of the four elements of fire, air, earth and water. Aristotle suggested a fifth element of ether, the element that fills the universe above the terrestrial plane, as he believed that the stars were possibly not made up of the elements found on Earth. Nowadays, we tend to think of the element of ether as that of spirit, that which exists beyond all physical matter.

Essentially, the elements also refer to the subtle

essence of the energies as well as the physical ones. That is, that the elements are not only physical but they also represent subtle energies. Earth represents solidity, water represents fluidity, fire represents temperature, air represents mobility and space represents expansiveness.

In meditation and conscious manifesting we can incorporate the four elements into our practice just as in any rituals, new and old. Fire is represented by the flame of the candle, and it can also represent our temperament. Air is represented by the incense, and also by our breath. Earth is represented by the act of grounding ourselves and also by paper (if we are writing our intentions). Water is represented by the ink used to write on the paper and a ritual bath (if we choose to bathe beforehand). Ether is represented by meditation to expand our consciousness.

Candles as a Focus for Divine Guidance

Candles have a practical and also an ancient purpose, such as those used in churches to represent the light of Christ or in ritual to represent one of the four elements. The candle offers a subtle light within which to work, and the lighting of the flame sets our intention. One can buy good-quality candles, and they come in many different colours. Beeswax candles are generally more expensive but are considered more empowering, as they are made from natural materials. Home-made candles are considered the most powerful to work with.

Working with candles is the simplest form of magic. A simple candle ritual is described in the section about working with the phases of the moon. Using candles as a focus can also be a wonderful way of connecting with angels.

Candles can be used as a focus of our faith, to connect with the light and angelic beings and to set our intent. When you light the candle, do so with the feeling in your heart of letting light and love into your life and connecting with the divine source.

Conscious Manifesting with Candles

Setting the Intent

If you are using a shop-bought candle you can set the intent of what the candle is to be used for and also clear away any negativity.

Hold the candle in both hands and visualise the white light passing through yours hands and clearing away any negativity that may be in the candle. You can ask your angels or spirit guides to assist. Ask that the candle is for positive intent (you may wish to state the intention) and that the workings you are undertaking are for the highest good of all. Give thanks.

Using Symbols

Now you can, if you wish, carve symbols into the candle. These can be reiki symbols, if you are a practitioner, or other familiar symbols such as love hearts, money symbols, runic symbols or others shapes symbolising the desires you wish to manifest. I like to carve my candles prior to dressing them, as it's easier.

Dressing

Next, you can dress your candle. I like to use pure essential oils to dress my candles, such as lavender, rosemary, frankincense, myrrh, spikenard, sandalwood or patchouli. Many of these oils were used in olden times and are found in the Bible and other ancient texts. You can use whatever oils resonate with you or a mixture of a couple of oils. The oils also add fragrance while burning, and put some of your energy into the candle. While dressing the candle, focus your intent on the purpose for which it is to be used.

Traditionally, candles can be dressed certain ways, and there are many variations. The oil can be rubbed from the top down to the middle. The oil can then be rubbed from the bottom to the middle. Some start at the middle and brush the oil to the top and then from the middle downwards. Do what feels right to you. As with all spiritual workings, intent is the key.

Candle Colours

Colours are associated with certain emotions and attributes, and so choosing the right coloured candle can add more emphasis to your work. However, if you don't have a certain colour, a white one can be used instead, as white contains all the other colours.

145

List of Colours and Associations

White	Red	Yellow
Spirituality	Energy	Intellect
Peace	Strength	Mental
Purity	Courage	Learning
	Goals	Creativity
	Health	Imagination
	Sexual energy	Memory

Pink	Green	Purple
Love	Abundance	Wisdom
Romance	Growth	Spiritual power
Nurturing	Luck	Higher psychic ability
Caring	Harmony	Material weath
	Fertility	
	Harvest	
	Nature	
	Physical healing	

Orange	Blue	Silver
General success	Protection	Clairvoyance
Career	Communication	Intuition
Ambition	Wisdom	Dreaming
Legal matters	Devotion	Astral travel
	Inspiration	

With the candle selected, cleansed, perhaps carved and then dressed, it can be then lit.

Now you can sit and meditate with it, visualising what you desire. Or you can write your wishes and intents on a piece of paper. Write your intents and wishes on to the paper and always add something along the lines of, 'This or something better, for the highest good of all.'

Remember, what we wish for is not always good for our spiritual journey. Adding this phrase is like an insurance policy, so that what we do get is good for us spiritually and harms no other. If, for example, we see a particular house that we want and it is available but a little above our price range, we may get the house, as we have put out to the universe that we want it. But then that purchase may turn into a financial or emotional disaster. It is better to manifest in a more open way, in that we want a new house but we are leaving it in the hands of the universe to direct us to that which serves our spiritual path and enriches our life rather than hinders it.

So now that we have written our desires, we have meditated and we have reflected on them, we can send them to the universe to manifest.

You will need a fireproof dish or container for this. The paper should be folded carefully, and lit by passing it over the candle flame. Once it is burning, carefully drop it into the flameproof dish. The embers can then be discarded by tossing them outside in the air (making sure that you are not facing the wind, or you'll get covered in ashes), tipped into the earth or tossed into a stream. It is up to you. Do what feels right.

Performing rituals such as this at certain moon phases adds even more power to your work (see the chapter on conscious manifesting with the moon).

To end the ritual, allow the candle to burn down entirely. Ensure that it is somewhere safe, in a suitable holder and that hot wax cannot drip on to surfaces that can be damaged or cause a fire.

Connecting with the Angels with Candles

Candles are a great way to focus for meditation and for angelic communication. Of course, angels can be contacted at any time, and the more you practise the easier it will get. There is something magical, however, about choosing a candle, lighting it and using it as a focus for angelic communication.

Here is a list of colours that can be used with angels. I have meditated on these and again. Intent is the key. This list is not set in stone, as sometimes the colours may flip. This means that a particular colour may resonate with you for a certain angel that is not on the list. Go with your intuition. These colours are for guidance and are not rigid.

White	Red	Yellow
Azrael	Gabriel	Jophiel
Metatron	Michael	Sandaphon
Zadkiel	Metatron	Uriel
		Zadkiel

Pink	Green	Purple
Chamuel	Ariel	Michael
Jeremiel	Raphael	Raziel
Jophiel		

Orange	Blue	Silver
Gabriel	Michael	Haniel
Raguel	Raphael	

Select the colour of candle and the name of the angel you wish to work with. Light the candle with the intention of connecting with the angel. You may wish to burn some incense or oils in a burner as well. Sit comfortably and take a few deep breaths.

Draw down the white light, a pure crystalline light, through the top of your head. Now visualise your aura expanding outwards as you ask for this connection to be made with your chosen angel. Focus on the candle flame as you connect. You may wish to say the name of the angel.

As you connect you may feel tickles on your face, a change in the air and a change in the energy of the room. You should always feel uplifted. If the energy feels heavy, ask it to go away and request that only beings of the pure light of God or of the divine source may enter your space. When you feel you have the connection, be aware of any impressions, images or words you may have. Notice how it feels. Stay with it for as long as you feel comfortable. If you do drift off, bring your focus back to the breath. Once you have finished, give thanks for your connection. Now write what you have experienced and how it felt in your journal.

Task

Try out some of the exercises and record in your journal how you feel and what experiences you have. Try connecting with the angels using the candles and record your findings.

Chapter 10

Creating Abundance

'Abundance is not something we acquire. It is something we tune into.'
Wayne Dyer.

One of the keys to success is the ability to have a positive approach to life and a good, positive self-image. Staying positive and on track is not always easy, as every one of us can go through challenging times at various points in our lives. These life events can drain our energy, hamper our progress or dampen our spirits. Life is not always a smooth path, but through life's challenges we can grow to be stronger and wiser.

At a time when I was younger and unwise, I found myself deeply in debt, virtually bankrupt and very, very depressed. I had two small children to look after, a failing business and debts that were spiralling out of control. I was so depressed I ended up under the care of a doctor and taking medication. It was truly the lowest point in my life.

One day, after six months of wallowing in a deep,

dark pit of depression, I literally woke up and decided to take my life back. I pleaded to God to show me the way. I decided that my life really wasn't meant to be like this.

It was from there that I committed myself to a daily meditation practice, usually when the children had gone to bed. From this, I developed on to positive thinking, goal setting and working with mantras, amongst other tools for self-development. My life began to change for the better, and although I still had many challenges, life seemed to drop into place. I may not be a millionaire but I have my own form of success and, above all else, happiness and contentment, which are more important than material things. Success means different things to different people. Success isn't just the about the acquisition of material things. It's a mindset.

The universe brings about many challenges and obstacles that we need to overcome so that we can evolve and grow. We live in an abundant universe and we all have within us the ability to live a happy and plentiful life.

I have had many challenges in my life, and have learnt to use various strategies in which to overcome them. Brought together here in one chapter are several tools that I have learnt to use along the way that can assist you in manifesting the life of your dreams. These have come together over many years of reading and compiling information. Most of all, I have used each one of these techniques to great success, and they are techniques that I use daily, weekly or monthly.

We have within us the ability to transcend the illusion of life to create our own reality, one greater than we could ever think possible. You have the ability within yourself to change your destiny for the better.

Being Grateful

Gratitude for what we have is something that tends to be overlooked. We can find ourselves focusing on the negatives rather than focusing on the positives. Instead, focusing on and expressing gratitude for what we do have, rather than on what we don't have, can bring about a more peaceful state. By expressing gratitude, we take away the focus from what we don't have and the stress and frustration that that brings. Expressing gratitude brings us into alignment with our authentic selves.

Once gratefulness begins to be embedded in everyday life and gratitude is given for what we have in life, the law of attraction takes effect. What we give out, we receive. Positive thoughts attract positive energies into our everyday existence. Gratitude is a vital element of success. Being grateful can eliminate some of the negative thoughts that can permeate daily life. Gratitude also brings more meaning to life. When you live in a state of gratitude the positive attitude it brings permeates through your life, and in turn attracts positive people and experiences.

I make gratitude part of my everyday life. When I decided to be more grateful for what I had rather than focus on my sense of lack, it changed my life for the better. I felt more positive, and better about myself and my circumstances. I attracted better people into my life. Sure, I seemed to piss people off with my positive attitude, but they were usually the sort of people who were always negative and tended to drag me down to their level. I was better off not being around those sorts of people.

Be grateful for everything in your life: your shower in the morning, the daily sunrise, the journey to work, your job, the food on the table, the weather, whatever money you have in your pocket, your family and your kids. The list is endless. It allows you to be in a state of mindfulness, to be aware of the possibilities, and it takes away some of the burdens of life.

At times, while on the way to work and wishing that I could be at home doing different things, I used to think to myself, 'I hate my job.' Most of us have been there. I changed that statement to, 'I am grateful for my job and the money it pays so that I can enjoy the nicer things in life.' My attitude to work changed, and I was happier and more successful at my work as a result.

Cultivating gratitude as a daily practice will bring you peace of mind, contentment and ultimately more abundance.

Journaling

'If your life's worth living, it's worth recording.'
Tony Robbins

Journaling is another tool to create an abundant mindset, to tap into creative processes and to set your goals and intentions. Sitting down with a journal, pen in hand, is an excellent way to review your day – seeing what went wrong and what could be done better, or setting your intentions for the day ahead and planning the day (depending on what time of the day you decide to journal). Writing in a journal can give valuable insights into your day that you may have never seen prior to writing things down.

The act of writing generally uses the left side of the brain, which is analytical. While this side of the brain is occupied, the right side of your brain, the creative side, is free to create. Writing can help release mental blocks to creativity and can help solve problems and clarify any challenges.

Recording in a journal helps formulate ideas and assists in tapping into the creative part of your brain. Many times when I write in my journal, thoughts and ideas pop into my head which I can then record for future reference. When reviewing an entry in your journal you may come across situations or ideas that you may have forgotten about. It's also nice to look back at the road travelled, from a place where you once were compared to where you are today. Reflection is a useful tool. It makes you think about what you did and why you did it, and can also help you to evaluate if it works. Subsequently, it helps identify plans that may need revising, or altering what no longer works for you. Use your journal to document ideas, insights, lessons learnt and, of course, successes.

Revisit that which you are grateful for. Write about what you appreciate: your goals, aspirations and positive affirmations. It need only take a few minutes each day. This can be in the morning, to set intentions and plan for the day, or at night, to review how the day went. I personally like to record and review the day's events. If it happens that I miss days, I write up all that I can remember or is important, reflecting and evaluating as I write.

Journaling helps gain clarity on issues and can allow you to work through problems. It can help you record goals and any ideas that you may have. These ideas can then be recorded for future use so that they are not forgotten. It can also help you review what worked and what didn't and help set new goals for the future. Journaling is useful in helping create a focus for success.

Meditation

The topic of meditation has been looked at in a previous chapter. It can also be used as a tool for success.

Luck can be perceived to be affected by mental processes, and this is where altering these mental processes, thoughts and attitudes to life can assist in improving your luck and abundance. An abundant mindset attracts just that: abundance in all its forms.

Meditation changes how the brainwaves react in the brain. During meditation the brainwaves change and some of these, such as alpha waves, are linked with deep relaxation and mental awareness. Regular meditators can shift into this more relaxed mode at will, which allows them to deal with stress efficiently. When your body and mind are calm, you can more easily access your intuition. This is where your creativity, hopes and dreams are stored. When you access this amazing source of wisdom that you've always had, you will be able to attract what you desire more easily. You will also be clearer on what you want to attract.

Meditation is a tool that can be used to attract what you desire in life. When you meditate regularly it lifts a veil from your mind's eye, allowing you to be more in tune with your circumstances and surroundings, seeing things perhaps with more clarity than you ever saw before.

Meditation can help tap into intuition and creativity, which in turn can attract abundance.

Start your own meditation practice daily. Just ten minutes of deep breathing and concentrating on your breath in a quiet place where you will not be disturbed is all you need to start with. As you get used to sitting in quiet contemplation, extend your time further. Twenty minutes a day is ideal, either in the morning or at night.

157

Positive Affirmations

We are, in essence, the product of our thoughts and the words that we repeatedly say to ourselves in our heads. We are the product of schooling, of what our family and friends have told us and the product of our environment. If we were brought up in a home where there was a sense of lack, we may carry that into our adult lives. If we are told that we are stupid, no good or useless, we can also carry those thoughts into adulthood.

What we chose to think and say from this moment on can mould our future into what we choose to create. We can change the persistent recordings in our heads from negative thoughts and fear into positive thoughts and actions. It can happen from this moment on.

Affirmations help change our mental programming. We are a result of the experiences that we have had up to this point in life, of what we have been told by others and of what we have told ourselves. The use of positive affirmations encourages gratitude and a positive attitude. Gratitude helps you to stay positive and to focus on positive things in your life.

Affirmations, when done correctly, are an effective tool in creating an abundant life, in helping us create who we want to be, and in assisting us to achieve what we wish to accomplish in life. They are positive statements that are worded in the present tense, never in the future or the past tense.

The godmother of positive affirmations is Louise L. Hay. To go further into the study of and working with positive affirmations I recommend reading her books. There is a wealth of information on the Internet on the subject of using affirmations, and plenty of positive affirmations to choose from.

A good tip is to find a positive affirmation to work with on a specific area of your life, which in this case may be abundance. You can write the affirmation in your journal and focus on it daily, or type it up and print it out with a relevant image or use of colour. You can even draw an image to go with it. Be as creative as you can. If, like me, you're not very artistic, you can search on the Internet and find many positive statements in the form of memes. These can be printed out and stuck up by your bed, on your vision board or displayed in a place where you can see them daily. Say them quietly to yourself and affirm that which you wish to create.

Using affirmations in this way can open new thinking pathways, which can help eliminate negative thought patterns or bad habits or help you create something new in your life. When using affirmations, remind yourself why you are using them. There's no point in reaffirming to yourself that you are abundant, then telling yourself that you are not and eventually giving up. Believe in what you are affirming to yourself.

Positive affirmations help keep you focused on what you want to achieve. With constant repetition you can eliminate feelings of doubt and insecurity. This can assist in making it easier to achieve a positive result.

If you are consistent with your use of affirmations and practice them daily, eventually changes will take place. Things won't change overnight. It takes patience. Think of it as putting your efforts out into the universe, and the universe then has to work on putting things into place to fulfil your desires. This takes time.

You can choose to change your thought patterns and the way you think. These choices can be put into action now.

Some examples of positive affirmations for abundance and success:

I am open to new and exciting opportunities, and they are revealed to me each day.

Abundance flows to me. I have more than enough money for all I want in life.

I am grateful for all the abundance that flows to me freely and effortlessly.

I am grateful that I have more than enough money to pay my bills and live an abundant life.

Money flows to me in endless abundance.

I am successful and abundant.

Money is a positive energy, and I focus on abundance.

I am open to new and wonderful possibilities, and my mind is free of resistance.

I am a spiritual and mental magnet to prosperity and success in every area of my life now.

I forget the mistakes of the past as I focus on my current successes.

I believe in myself and my ability to achieve.

I am a successful and prosperous person.
I attract abundance and prosperity in all its forms.
I constantly attract new and exciting opportunities.
Prosperity and abundance flow to me freely and
easily.
I choose success and happiness.
I am prosperous, healthy and happy.
I am blessed with health, wealth and happiness in
all areas of my life now.
I am a spiritual and mental magnet, attracting
to myself all things that bless me and make me
prosper.
I am a wonderful success in all my undertakings
and am happy.
Every day in every way I am getting better and
better.

These are all examples of positive affirmations to use for abundance. The list is not exhaustive, and it should be able to give you some starters. There are many other affirmations that you can use to find love, to heal relationships, to heal your mind and body and to release bad habits that hold you back in life. There are a variety of resources available in books and on the Internet. Use what resonates well with you.

Goal Setting

This chapter wouldn't be complete without a section on goal setting. Here's the conundrum:
   Do spiritual people just drift through life and hope

to achieve what they set out to do? Or is there scope for the spiritual individual to actually plan and set goals to achieve success?

I've always planned and achieved things that I never thought possible. Then a very close spiritual friend suggested that I shouldn't set goals; that I was right where I was meant to be in life. In a way I agree, but it's too easy to fall into a trap of just drifting through life and reaching a certain age and thinking, 'Where did all those years go? I still haven't achieved this or that.'

So, for a few years, I set no goals and drifted with no direction. I sat and waited for opportunities to come my way. Time passed. I got frustrated that nothing happened. So I went back to my goal setting habits and, like a miracle, things began to happen, to move, to shift in the direction I wanted. I became more focused on my intentions.

Goal setting is an important tool for success. Goals create a focus for where you want to be in life. By setting goals one can give more emphasis and focus to achieving certain things. They don't have to be materialistic. They could be spiritual. What are your goals for one year from now, for five years from now or even for ten years from now? Goal setting is another tool in the toolbox of conscious manifesting. Successful people set goals. Goals give the focus towards the dreams you have. Setting goals directs the attention and gives you something to work towards. They give direction, something to strive for and ultimately self-satisfaction when the goal is achieved. It's only a dream until you write it down. Then it becomes a goal. So go on – set those goals.

Here are some pointers to set you off:

* ❖ Goal statement – What is your goal? Identify it. Be specific.
* ❖ Why is this goal important to you? – Identify why the goal is important.
* ❖ Actions you need to put in place to achieve your goal – List the action steps you need to take. Break the big picture into small steps. Set a time by which you wish to complete each action. For example, can they be done immediately? In a month? In a year?
* ❖ Skills and resources needed – What skills do you need to achieve your goal? What resources do you need?
* ❖ What obstacles I may face? – Identify the obstacles that may hinder progress. A lack of money or of resources? Maybe it's an emotional block, such as fear. Identify them.
* ❖ How can I overcome these obstacles? – What do you need to overcome those obstacles? To improve your skills? To generate more clients?
* ❖ My reward when I achieve my goal – Set yourself a reward. There is no greater joy than in realising a goal, which in turn builds self-confidence. Plan a reward, no matter how small.

So, write those goals down. Revisit them regularly. Make new goals when the old ones have been achieved. Rethink and revise goals if they don't seem to be working out.

Setting goals can be a wonderful tool, which can help you achieve great things in your life.

Creating a Vision Board

Vision boards are a collection of images and perhaps phrases that reflect what you envision your life should be or what you want to achieve. For example: a new kitchen, a new home, happiness, family unity, career success, a beautiful garden, a holiday.

Vision boards can be drawn using lots of images and colour, pictures from magazines or catalogues or images printed from the Internet.

The optimum time to create a vision board is around the time of the new moon (see the chapter on conscious manifesting with the moon). This is a traditional time in the moon's cycle to manifest desires. It can be done on the actual day of the new moon or the first few days following the new moon.

By making a vision board you are creating a sacred space that displays what you want in life. Visualisation is a powerful tool to use in manifesting desires. When you create a vision board and display it in a place where you can see it often you are creating a visualisation experience whenever you cast your eyes upon it.

A vision board should focus not only on what you want but also how you want to feel. The more your board focuses on how you want to feel the more energy is put into your vision and the more it will come to life.

Anything can be put on to your vision board that inspires you. Areas to cover may be finance, health and well-being, relationships, the home and personal growth. There is no need, however, to cover all these areas. Focus on areas that have meaning to you. There is no wrong or right way to create a vision board.

Task: Create a Vision Board

You will need:

- ❖ A corkboard, a poster board or a large sheet of card.
- ❖ Pins, scissors, a glue stick or sticky tape, coloured pens and pencils if you're arty.
- ❖ Magazines, catalogues, printed images from the Internet, phrases, sayings, inspirational quotes, photos.

How to do it:

The most important thing is to set time aside in which to create. Preferably it will be around the time of the new moon, which gives it more power, or at a waxing phase of the moon. Set aside one or two hours when you won't be disturbed. Put on some gentle music, burn incense, or put some oils in a diffuser if you wish. The choice is yours. Lay everything out before gluing or pinning it. I like to cover my board so that there are no spaces. Most of all, be creative and let the ideas flow. When you've finished, display your vision board in a prominent place where you will see it every day.

Chapter 11

Mantras for Success

'You are a cosmic flower. Om chanting is the process of opening the psychic petals of that flower.'
Amit Ray

Mantras are, in essence, a form of ancient positive affirmation that are repeated over and over to manifest or achieve a particular goal. They are short phrases, usually in the ancient language of Sanskrit, which direct energy to manifest a particular intention. Sanskrit is an ancient language used in Hinduism. Today it is used in Hindu ceremonies, rituals and in mantras and is considered a phonetic language, although it is now defunct as an everyday language.

Mantras can be used to help assist with the problems we face in life. They are a tool in our toolbox that can be used to smooth the challenges we face, but they are not the only or the best way to solve problems. Our karma, the law of cause and effect, our accumulated thoughts, our actions and our environment all play a part in dictating the point at which we are in life and the path we are currently on. Your energy, thoughts, words and deeds culminate to trigger your experiences. Mantras, however, are extremely powerful in assisting us on our path and smoothing the way ahead, and can help solve some problems.

Mantras can help overcome problems in life and can assist in making massive changes. They are a tool for healing. Repetition of a mantra can be used as a focus for meditation, can help release a habitual mindset and can release karmic bonds. It can help alter spiritual and physical energy patterns, as mantras are energy-based sounds. The vibrational sound of the mantra works on the chakra system and energises prana, our basic life force energy. The combination of repeating the sound of the mantra, together with intention, amplifies the energetic effect of the mantra and increases it's intensity.

Mantras are extremely powerful, and are not to be underestimated. They possess the power to shift energetic blocks very quickly. As such one should be mindful that, when using mantras, a healing crisis can occur, or blocks that may arise that disrupt your practice. Examples of these may be: coming down with a sudden cold, headaches, generally feeling unwell or being irritable. Blocks can arise whereby you may find it difficult to complete your mantra work. This could be a disruption of some sort, or an urgent matter that takes you away from your daily discipline. When these things happen, you know that your mantra is working, as you are beginning to encounter some form of inner resistance. As with all energy work, shifts can manifest in various forms.

There is a vast array of mantras and variations that one can choose from. In this section are a few that address various life issues, including luck and abundance. Strictly speaking, any mantra will do. Choose one that resonates the most.

Getting Started

In essence, just about any mantra will do. Go through the various mantras and pick one to work with, one that resonates well with you. If you wish, you can ask for divine guidance to assist you in achieving your objective, the goal that you wish to achieve while completing your mantra discipline. There are a few approaches to completing your mantra work.

I have used mantras very successfully over the years. They can be very transformative. There are two basic ways in which to use mantras.

1. You can repeat your mantra over a period of time, repeating it as often as possible. You can say the mantra repeatedly while cleaning, while in the shower or while taking the dog for a walk. Be mindful if you say the mantra while driving or doing anything technical. If you get spacey it may be dangerous, so stop immediately. If you wish to keep track of how many times you have said it, record it in a notebook. Record how many times you say it in a minute. Record how many minutes you have completed in your practice, and you should have a good estimate.

This type of practice is generally completed over a twenty-one-day cycle.

2. Alternatively, the traditional way for practising mantras, according to Eastern texts, is for forty days. You should decide a time when and a place where you can repeat your mantra. Mantras are generally repeated using a mala of 108 beads. You would use this to repeat the mantra in repetitions of 108. One can specifically use a mala or, like I do, a rosary. The rosary has fifty-four beads on it, minus the pendant, and this is a half mala. Therefore, two rounds on the rosary will give you 108 repetitions. The mantra can be practised in the morning or the evening or both. One mala of 108 repetitions a day can suffice but the more effort you put in, the more dramatic the results can be. Decide on how many malas you can do each day. When I have undertaken a mantra discipline in the past I have recorded how many repetitions I have done for each day in my journal, and therefore have kept a track of how many days have been completed. Endeavour to complete your practice without interruption.

Another alternative is if you wish to use two mantras at once. One mantra can be used in the morning for a set number of malas, and another mantra can be used in the evening. This would be completed over a period of forty days.

Every mantra I have ever worked with as a forty-day discipline has always started off well. Then, part way through, some blocks have occurred, such as coming down with a cold, feeling tired and grumpy, or oversleeping so I couldn't complete my morning mala.

Once I undertook a mantra discipline which would help me to connect more fully to my guide. I practised for forty days with no hiccups and nothing getting in the way of my practice. On the very last day of my discipline, Day Forty, I successfully completed what I set out to do. For the first time, I thought nothing had happened to take me away from my practice. I'd successfully completed my mantras, and I hadn't had any feelings of irritability or feeling unwell. That morning the sun was shining, the birds were singing and I felt amazing. It was a beautiful day in May, and I literally skipped to work that morning.

As I got into the office, my manager challenged me over a file that I had accidentally left at home. She was rude, aggressive and slammed papers on the desk. It wasn't a particularly important file. It was one that could be handed in the next day. As I found out later, other colleagues handed their files in up to three weeks later than me. I was summoned into the office of my head of area, who was absolutely lovely, and asked if there was anything that she could do to help. I explained that the file was up to date and it would be fine if it was given to my line manager the next day. I also handed in my notice there and then.

To say she was shocked was an understatement, but I knew it was the right thing to do. The relief I felt from resigning from my stressful teaching job was overwhelming. I never regretted my decision and have never looked back. Since that day I have never been happier at work, and I reverted to a less stressful role within the college where I worked.

Even when something that may be perceived as negative happens, it could actually be clearing the way for positive changes and manifesting things that you never even considered previously.

Some Simple Mantras

The following are simple mantras that you can use. The translations and pronunciations come from the work of Thomas Ashley-Farrand (now unfortunately deceased) and his book Healing Mantras 1, the most transformative book I have ever read. I am eternally grateful for his work.

Om Gum Ganapatayei Namaha
OM GUM GUH-NUH-PUH-TUH-YEI NAHM-AH-HA

The rough translation for this mantra is: 'Om and salutations to the remover of obstacles for which Gum is the seed.'

This is the mantra that removes obstacles on your path, and is by far my favourite mantra to use. There may be many blocks on your path, seen and unseen, and this is a wonderful mantra to clear the way to success in all endeavours. It's gentle yet powerful, and I often chant it while driving to work. It smooths the path ahead. It can remove obstacles in relationships as well as creating abundance, and is a good all-round mantra to work with.

Om Shrim Mahalakshmiyei Swaha
OM SHREEM MAH-HA LAHKSH-MEE-YEI SWAHA

The rough translation for this mantra is: 'Om and salutations to that feminine energy which bestows all manner of wealth and for which Shrim is the seed.'

This mantra can be used to achieve abundance in any form. It not only attracts prosperity but can also be used to attract suitable friends, assist with health issues and clear up misunderstandings with family. When using this mantra, have a clear focus on what you want to achieve. Ideally this mantra would be used on a classic forty-day discipline, but I have often used chanted this mantra on the way to work or for a period of time, especially when things have been tight financially. I've never ceased to be amazed by the extra bit of money that has come my way out of the blue and from unexpected sources. Sometimes it has come by way of being asked to do extra hours at work, immediately after chanting this mantra while driving to work in the morning. Wealth, remember, comes in many different forms.

Om Namah Shivaya
OM NAH-MAH SHEE-VAH-YAH

This mantra has no rough translation. It utilises the elements which govern the chakras: earth, fire, water, air and ether.

This mantra is good for general self-empowerment and for spiritual growth. When you chant this mantra, see yourself becoming perfect in your own way. I find it effective at clearing away etheric debris and clearing away negativity.

Om Sharavana Bhavaya Namaha
OM SHAH-RAH-VAH-NAH BHAH-VAH-YAH NAHM-AH-HA

The rough translation of this mantra is: 'Om and salutations to the son of Shiva, who brings auspiciousness and who is chief of the celestial army.'

This is a form of good luck mantra, and it can help bring about good outcomes from various circumstances. It can help increase a positive emotional or mental disposition, increase good luck or good fortune and assist in an easier path to physical fitness. It appears to brighten and enhance just about anything in life.

Om Eim Saraswatyei Swaha
OM I'M SAH-RAH-SWAH-TEE-YEA SWAH-HAH

The rough translation of this mantra is: 'Om and salutations to that feminine energy which informs all artistic and scholastic endeavours and for which Eim is the seed.'

This mantra is good for anyone pursuing an educational, musical or artistic venture. For anything which involves being creative, this is a very good mantra for making it successful. I used this mantra while undertaking two degrees back to back. It seemed to help me concentrate and complete my work effectively.

Om Sri Shanaishwaraya Swaha
OM SHREE SHAHN-EHSH-WAHR-EYE-YAH SWAH-HA

The rough translation of this mantra is: 'Om and salutations to the presiding spirit in the planet Saturn.'

Saturn is the planet of lessons that we learn in life. Saturn works in a specific way triggering karma. Through repetition of Sanskrit mantras you have the ability to change your karma. The whole idea behind spiritual disciplines is to assist in changing or reducing karma. It can help smooth your path in life and assist in understanding the lessons given to you in your lifetime. When I first started to use this mantra I struggled with it initially as it cleared away energetic imbalances, but eventually it smoothed my path and I could work with it with ease.

Om Mani Padme Hum
OM MAH-NEE PAHD-MEY HOOM.

This commonly known mantra is often translated as: 'The jewel of consciousness is in the heart's lotus.'

This mantra gives the precept that the heart and mind are united as one. It can be used to enhance compassion, and this can assist in manifesting in subtle and obvious ways. It is wonderful for spiritual advancement. No section on mantras would be complete without the addition of this wonderful and most repeated mantra in the world.

Task

Think of an area of life that you wish to improve and/or select a mantra that resonates with you. Find a quiet place in which to repeat your mantra for a number of malas and continue this practice for forty days, noting any effects it has. You may wish to purchase a mala of 108 beads, a rosary, or even make your own mala to use for your practice. Or alternatively, recite your mantra as much as possible for twenty-one days. Keep a record of how many times you have recited it, if you can, and how it makes you feel. Make a note of any results you may have.

Reference

◈ Ashley-Farrand, T., *Healing Mantras*, (1999), Random House, USA.

Chapter 12

My Story

The reason for sharing this story is to reveal how I came to this point in my life. It hasn't been an easy journey. Events in life tend to push us in the direction that is needed at the time. They put us on a path towards understanding why things happen the way they do, and the direction in which these experiences push us in life.

When I look back on my life it makes me realise how I became the person I am today. I had a difficult start to life, but I know that I chose my parents and experiences prior to my incarnation in this life. My life experiences make me who I am, and I am grateful for them. It is because of my life experiences that I have been continually pushed on the spiritual path. Various experiences throughout my life have led me on to the path that I am on today. It has been a journey of self-discovery and, more importantly, self-healing.

Mum left when I was nine months old. Dad, at the time, was in The Christie, Manchester, being treated for cancer. At one point, he was down to six and a half stone in weight and had been given the last rites.

Mum left for reasons that have often been speculated about, but ultimately I will never know why. I don't blame my mother. In my quest to find that answer, and meaning to my life, these experiences put me on the spiritual path that I am on today. When I was younger, however, it left me bitter, with a very large chip on my shoulder that took years of self-development and self-discovery to get rid of.

No one knows the reasons why Mum left. Thankfully Dad pulled through. As a result, and unusually for the time, Dad was awarded full custody of me. This was to be a start for the difficulties I would experience.

Mother leaving was a catalyst for other events that occurred in my early life. Dad found a partner who hit me quite a bit. She had no patience for me. That relationship subsequently broke up. I was already a broken child but I retreated, withdrawn and shy, even more into my shell. Then Dad met his second wife. Hermione. In the beginning it was wonderful. She was like my best friend, and we had so much fun together.

In 1977 we moved from Chorley to a new house in Leyland, a nearby town. Until this point I had seen my mother every other weekend. Once we had moved I never saw Mum again, till many years later at my maternal grandfather's funeral. For whatever reason, I was stopped from seeing him as well. I had been close to my granddad when I was little, and loved spending time with him. My memories of him were of him playing tunes on his piano and hiding behind his sofa when Doctor Who was on television. He promised that one day he would teach me to play the piano. That day never came.

I had an extremely difficult start to my life, and as a result I was a very lonely child. My paternal grandmother, Nanna, as I called her, looked after me for the most part. She was an alcoholic, experienced social anxiety and had a hoarding disorder. Despite her difficulties, she looked after me the best way she could and gave me the love I needed. She taught me to read and write before I started school.

Because of her difficulties, when I was at Nanna's she wouldn't let me play out with the other kids. This added to my loneliness and my feeling of being isolated. My only salvation was school, which I absolutely loved. I adored spending my time with other kids, and relished being at school in my younger years.

When I look back, I realise now that perhaps being kept away from socialising with other kids made my mindset different to that of a lot of other people. One day at junior school (a Roman Catholic school) the teacher told us that we could talk to God anytime we wanted. I was thrilled. Every morning when I walked to school I talked to God, and told him all my problems and discussed my day. I was about eight at the time. It took away my sense of loneliness, knowing that I could talk to someone. I never had a sense of God answering back, but I took comfort in knowing that a being was there to listen.

My new stepmum Hermione treated me as her own

child to begin with. I felt loved, and she was like my best friend. It wasn't to last. We moved to a village called Adlington when I was ten. I made friends there, and for the first time my deep sense of loneliness was alleviated. But this move was to be the start of new problems.

Hermione became pregnant. The paternity of this child was unknown. After the baby was born things went from bad to worse. Hermione, it transpired, had had a drink and drug abuse problem as a college student. This problem was to resurface and stay with her for the remainder of her adult life. Hermione gradually became more and more dependent on alcohol. She became more and more abusive to me. Instead of hitting me, she used psychological abuse.

Hermione turned her spite on to me, telling me most days that I was ugly, thick and useless. I wasn't allowed to eat the same foods as everyone else and all my clothes were second-hand and ill-fitting, whereas her child got all new clothes. I went to school with a badly fitting uniform and shoes that were a size too big. She went out of her way to make me feel as worthless as possible.

My dad at this time was working long hours to pay for her alcohol addiction. I wasn't given money to get the bus home, so she would often leave me waiting for half an hour to an hour for her to pick me up. When she eventually did, she was verbally abusive. The kids at high school soon picked up on the fact that I had issues. I was badly bullied, especially when some of the kids found out about Hermione's alcoholism and my Nanna's difficulties. One day one of the kids told the rest of the group that it was no wonder I was a weirdo because the rest of my family were weird.

Hermione had many affairs with various men in the village. Word soon got about.

One day my dad decided enough was enough and we moved back to Nanna's. I was thirteen. It was like I was released from prison. Dad however, lost everything. All we had between us was a bed, a wardrobe, a mirror and a portable telly. This time was a catalyst for both of us. My dad rebuilt his life, remarried and is now comfortably well-off and happy. I've also been blessed with a lovely stepbrother.

When I was fifteen years of age, I turned. I think that I'd just had enough. I ended up having a scrap after school with a girl who constantly bullied me. I was absolutely petrified, but stood my ground. I came away with a fat lip. After finally standing up for myself, the kids at school began to leave me alone. Somehow, I was no longer a weak and feeble misfit who could be easily picked on and bullied.

Suddenly I gained a new sense of adventure and a confidence in myself that I never had before. I started to socialise more, gain new friends and express my new-found confidence through music, fashion, make-up and hairstyles. I was drawn into social drinking with my friends and the clubbing scene (going clubbing was very prevalent in the eighties). Wrapped up in my hedonistic lifestyle, I forgot about my experiences with the spiritual side of life and sought my own pleasures.

I went off the rails for a number of years and became a bit of a wild child. I left home at eighteen and never went back. It was during my clubbing days that I met my future husband, Mark. I was out with my best friend Sara in a bar in our stomping ground of Chorley. Sara spotted a lad called Dave across the bar. Dave was on a night out with Mark. All four of us hooked up and walked away from the bar to get a taxi home. As we were walking along we were attacked from behind by two lads. Mark nearly ended up crashing through a florist's shop window and smashed his head on the wall at the edge of the window. Concerned for his welfare, we put him in a taxi home. After that night, Mark and I were inseparable. We had an immediate connection. Sara married Dave; I married Mark. We found our soulmates that eventful evening. It was destiny.

We've had our ups and downs but Mark and I have been together for a long time and have two wonderful boys, of whom we're so proud.

I forgot all about my spirituality until after I had my son, Conor. I decided that I needed to get back in shape so my friend and I decided to go to a Muay Thai boxing club at a local leisure centre. I'd always loved martial arts. I had spent many hours at my grandmother's watching a programme on the television called *Kung Fu*, starring David Carradine.

The Muay Thai classes not only helped me to keep fit but also to get rid of pent up aggression. I was extremely insecure, and because of my life experiences I still had a huge chip on my shoulder. The first night

I got there I was so nervous. I was terrified. Those classes, however, once I got over my initial nerves, gave me a new sense of freedom and built my self-confidence. They also, rather strangely, got me back in touch with my spirituality.

One day, while sparring with the champion fighter, he punched me on the nose and I lost my temper. My fists and legs were flying around all over the place. Afterwards Dave told me that in losing my temper my energy was all over the place, and I had to learn to channel this energy through to the ends of my fists and feet. Channelling energy... Wow. This one moment – this one conversation – led me to my life's work. Dave didn't know, but he was to change my life forever and I'm eternally indebted to him. Spiritual teachers come in many forms. They may come from many walks of life and express what they have to say in the humblest of terms. And what they tell you may not be obvious until you reflect on the wisdom and guidance they give, at the time when you most need it.

I began to purchase all the books I could on Buddhism and meditation, and began meditating on a regular basis. These books taught me about directing and working with energy. This in turn led me in later years to directing and channelling energy in my healing work, which is what I do to this day. It's something that I have carried on through life.

I meditate for around twenty minutes every day, mostly in the mornings. When I finish my meditation, I send out healing to my family and to those who need it and I also colour my path for the day. Buddhists believe that one year's worth of meditation practice daily equates to five years' life experience.

As I started to expand on my meditation practice, spiritual energies began to come through more often. Sometimes a spirit would speak to me at unexpected times. Whenever I meditated, visions of Native Americans would appear in my mind's eye. They came through so vividly that I could hear their chanting. This would happen for a number of years.

Life went on, and I had a second child. I wandered a little off the spiritual path as my meditation practice dwindled.

After I had my second child it was the darkest time of my life. We were virtually bankrupt, with a baby and a small child. Very little money was available, and I felt helpless.

I experienced postnatal depression and it felt like a deep, dark pit from which I could not escape. Thank fully I received the medical help that I needed. This experience made me question life and what it meant, as during this time I had suicidal thoughts. The darkest part of my life put me on the path to healing.

It was at this time that I began to get interested in positive affirmations as a way of changing my negative mindset. I bought a book on using affirmations and I worked with them, repeating them over and over as often as I could. Slowly, things began to change and my mental health began to improve. We got rid of the shop that we had at that time, and I put my trust in the universe to assist in changing my life for the better. As if by a miracle, through word of mouth, I immediately got work as a waitress and my husband got temporary work with an agency and then a permanent position with the Royal Mail. We never looked back.

To get myself through my depression I connected more fully with my meditation practice. With what little money I had I bought as many books as I could on self-help and spirituality. I began to feel more confident about myself as my depression lifted.

In 1998, I undertook a spiritual healing course that had a professionally recognised qualification. I saved what money I could from my waitressing work and continued my studies, learning holistic therapies. I qualified in various types of massage, and in reflexology and aromatherapy. I got some work in various complementary therapy centres, but the universe had different plans for me. By this time, I had left my job as a waitress.

I took a voluntary position at a local college as a learning support worker, working with young adults with learning difficulties. I absolutely adored my role and was thankful to secure a paid role with the college. This set me on the path to completing a degree in biology and then my teaching degree, which I did while still working part time and looking after my small family. I had an inner strength and a desire to complete my degrees successfully. It was almost as if some unseen force was pushing me to complete my work.

I taught foundation studies for a few years,

combining my role of learning support worker for half the week and teaching for the other half. Eventually I gave up teaching, but when this came about I had decided to embrace the spiritual path again. However, my teaching experience gave me the skills to deliver, plan and teach healing and workshops.

After completing my degrees, I went through some personal difficulties. I was rather forcefully pushed back on to the spiritual path by some unseen force.

One day, when I was feeling down, I called in at the local coffee shop, where the owner did readings and spiritual development classes. I had a reading with Julie and she invited me to start on her spiritual awareness class, which was being held the next month. She became my spiritual teacher and I am so blessed, as she taught me so much. One weekend, in 2010, she was teaching an angel workshop. I was at a low point with my relationship difficulties. That day changed my life. I connected with the angels at a much deeper level than I had ever experienced before.

You see, I had forgotten my angels. Having gone to a Catholic school and being brought up in the Catholic Church, even though no one else in my family was Catholic (my mum was, but of course she'd left), I had learnt to talk to God and, according to the Catholic faith, we were assigned guardian angels. So I was aware of angels but until this point I hadn't really connected with them or really accepted them into my life, even though I knew they were there. It was as if I had forgotten them. Throughout my life, I have always been able to see and sense spirit as well as having a sense of the angelic realm. As a small child, I would often wake up to see a spirit sitting on my bed. Many people would be freaked out by this but I was used to it happening. It was a regular occurrence for me that doesn't happen as often now.

I bought any angel book I could get my hands on. I became an avid fan of Doreen Virtue, as I found her work easy to digest. I needed more, however. One of the members of Julie's development group, Alison, knew a lady who taught reiki and who was deeply connected to the angels. This person, Yvonne, became my second spiritual teacher, and through her I became attuned to angelic Usui reiki. When I was attuned, the energies were so amazing. I cannot put into words how I felt each time I had my attunements. Reiki is very different to spiritual healing, as it uses symbols. I have found it to be much more powerful and a much more spiritual experience, both for the practitioner and the recipient.

My angelic healing and meditation classes, led by Yvonne, were something else, and opened up a whole new world of angelic communication.

There is a saying that when the student is ready the teacher will appear. When the time was right two spiritual teachers appeared on my path. The right teachers came along at the right time.

Throughout my years spent developing my gifts, I constantly asked for my guide to reveal himself or herself. It took many years before my guide was revealed to me.

Julie held regular meditation classes in her shop every

Thursday morning. Because of work commitments, I could only go during to her classes during the holidays.

One Thursday morning in August, I went to Julie's meditation class. We started the session off with a white light meditation to relax the group and to connect. Then we started the visualisation that Julie guided us through. It was to connect us with our guide. What I received was profound.

My guide came through to me in the meditation. He appeared to me in a loose, Arabic-style long tunic or kaftan in plain cloth. He lifted his long sleeves to reveal his arms to me. They were covered in tattoos, which looked like symbols. He held up his right hand, on which was a tattoo of an eight-pointed star. It was the star of Ishtar, as I subsequently discovered after some research. He told me that I was originally a star child from the Pleiades, although I had had many incarnations on the Earth plane. My guide was of Mesopotamian origin and he eventually gave the name Ür. However, this name came to me some time after.

When I came through the meditation I realised how profound it was. There was a reason why my guide had not revealed himself to me previously. Before this time, I was not spiritually ready and probably would not have been able to understand or deal with the information that I was given. Since this time Ür has come back to me many times. I know that we have walked the desert together in a previous lifetime. The tattoos on his arm are a mystery to me, but I'm sure one day their meaning will be revealed.

Sometimes now while meditating I'm given profound information. When I opened up psychically six years ago it was at a more advanced level that I had experienced previously. I believe that, as each year passes, I am opening up more and more as I progress on the spiritual path.

All kinds of bizarre things began to happen at this time as I opened up more fully. The doorbell would mysteriously ring as I or my husband was pulling on or off the drive in our cars. I believe this happened so that we knew for sure that it was not down to kids playing tricks by ringing the doorbell and running away, as either one of us could confirm that no one was at the door. The television would switch itself on at night at various times when we were asleep, or the microwave would bleep on its own. To some this may seem a bit scary, but to me it was reassurance that I was opening up spiritually and psychically and that I had unseen helpers around. A lot of this activity has now died down as I follow my spiritual path more, although it still happens now and again.

In 2010, we lost Mary, my mother-in-law, Mark's mum. It was one of the hardest things I had to get through in my adult life. Mary had problems with drinking too much after losing her husband. She filled up her lonely void with alcohol and became withdrawn from the world. Eventually she barely went out. I would take her shopping each week, because her mobility had become quite poor.

That year her health took a turn for the worse. We had no idea what was up with her. Ironically, she'd cut down her drinking, but her mobility was getting worse and worse. She was lethargic and couldn't move very far. Even though the doctor's surgery was at the bottom of the street I had to drive her there as her legs couldn't carry her. The doctor refused to do anything for her, which I assumed was due to her record of alcoholism. A day later, I called the doctor's again for a house visit. He looked at her and said there was nothing he could do as there were no visible signs of illness, but prescribed an ointment for a skin rash she had. We called the doctor's again a few days later. It was a Friday. The doctor refused to walk up the street to see her and diagnosed her by phone.

On the Saturday evening, we got a call from Mary. She was unable to get herself upstairs to bed. I helped her upstairs and helped get her nightgown on. She had to be lifted into bed. Then she started to vomit. It was brown in colour. I was unaware at the time that the vomit was brown due to blood. I called the out of hours doctor, who came straight away. It was his last evening on the job before retiring. He rang for an ambulance for her. The relief was enormous. I wept and thanked him. I knew now she could get treatment for whatever condition she had.

Days later she was dead. She died of a skin infection that had got into her internal organs.

When she was unconscious, a day before she died, I asked the angels to surround her bed and give her comfort. I saw in my mind's eye a host of angels around her bed, giving comfort to her failing body. The next day she passed away. We spent sixteen hours by her bed, waiting for her spirit to pass. As a family, we were absolutely devastated. She was the closest thing I had ever had to a mother. She never judged me and always accepted me for who I was. She took me into her home at a time in my life when I was eighteen and had nowhere else to go. I was and still am forever indebted to her.

Whenever I see flashes of light, I know angels are near. Before Mary's death I continually saw flashes of violet and purple lights. I knew that the angels were with us.

What I am more aware of is that I have been connecting more fully with my guide and with the angels in recent years. Prior to this I believed that I was fully connected to the spiritual realm. I was not. I was only partially awake, partially connected. Even now I know that there are more areas in which I can develop as I travel on my spiritual path. There is still much to develop, still much to improve.

Over the years I have had many experiences with spiritual entities. One day, while walking in some local woods, I stopped to sit and meditate on a bench with my friend. As I sat there, connecting with nature, it was as if the woodland was coming alive. I could feel lots of little eyes peering at us as we sat on the bench. As I looked into the sunlight-dappled woodland and foliage, I thought I could make out little creatures moving around just out of the corner of my eye. I closed my eyes once more as I connected with nature. The atmosphere seemed as though it was charged with electricity. Then, as I opened my eyes once more, I saw a small creature jump on to my knee. It seemed about five inches tall. I let out a shriek, as I was startled, but when I looked closely there was nothing there. I believe that I had connected with the fairy realm, and what I saw in the corner of my eye was a fairy. It was a truly magical experience.

A few years prior to this I participated in a ghost hunt in woodland overnight, less than a mile away from that place. There, as a group, we experienced many strange phenomena. One of the group was taking photos with her digital camera all night, capturing orbs and strange, misty formations. She shouted me over to look at an image she had taken of a tree just before dawn. She increased the magnification, and there at the bottom of the tree were what appeared to be three little people. I was blown away. I couldn't believe my eyes. She still has the picture somewhere.

I went from a non-believer to believing in the existence of fairies. I believe that there exist alternate realms of beings who we are not able to see in our physical plane, who reside in a non-physical alternate dimension and that these physical and non-physical realms exist side by side.

Another time I visited a relative who has a large house in the countryside. To make use of the countryside views, the house has been built upside down, if you will, in that the bedrooms are downstairs and the living room and kitchen are on the first floor, with another bedroom In the attic space.

I stood in the living room looking across at the trees and the surrounding countryside, admiring the view, as it was a beautiful, sunny day. Suddenly, out of the foliage of one of the trees, a face appeared – a face full of green leaves, with strings of leaves coming out from either side of its mouth. The face came right out of the tree's green foliage. It was a green man, and looked just as a green man is traditionally depicted. I was taken aback. Silently, I said, 'Thank you,' and the face went back into the tree. Again, I was being shown nature spirits. This time they were the nature spirit of the tree, spirits that exist beyond our perception of the physical plane.

When I look back at my life's experiences I am never sad or bitter as I know that they have been put on my path for a reason, as an opportunity to learn, grow and evolve. Through my experiences I can help others along the way.

There is no past, no future. There is, and always will be, only the present moment.

Life is a journey full of wonder. No matter what time of life you find yourself at as you open up to the spiritual aspect of yourself – whether you are young or old – life contains such joy, excitement and wonder. Experience it in all its richness and complexity.

I am truly grateful for all that I was and for all that I will be.

Bibliography and Further Reading

Andrews, T., *How to Meet and Work with Spirit Guides*, (1992), Minnesota, USA, Llewellyn Publications.

Andrews, T., The Healer's Manual: *A Beginner's Guide to Energy Healing for Yourself and Others,* (2011), Minnesota, USA, Llewellyn Publications.

Ashley-Farrand, T., *Healing Mantras: Using Sound Affirmations for Personal Power, Creativity, and Healing*, (1999), Ballantine Wellspring, USA.

Buckland, R., *Practical Candle Burning: Spells and Rituals for Every Purpose,* (2003), Minnesota, USA, Llewellyn Publications.

Cooper, D., *Angel Inspiration: How to Change Your World with the Angels*, (2004), London, Hodder & Stoughton.

Elrod, H., Petrini, P., *The Miracle Morning for Network Marketers*, (2015), Great Britain, Hal Elrod International.

Gawain, S., *Creative Visualization*, (2002), Canada, Publishers Group West.

Hay, L., *Heal Your Body*, (2007), London, Hay House UK Ltd.

James, U., *The Source: A Manual of Everyday Magic,* (2011), London, England, Preface Publishing.

Malachi, T., Houston, S., *Gnostic Healing: Revealing the Hidden Power of God*, (2010), Minnesota, USA, Llewellyn Publications.

Malachi, T., *Gnosis of the Cosmic Christ: A Gnostic Christian Kabbalah*, (2011), Minnesota, USA, Llewellyn Publications.

Nyland, A., Dr., *Angels, Archangels and Angel Categories; What the Ancients Said*, (2010), Queensland, Australia, Smith and Sterling.

Ozaniec, N., *The Elements of the Chakras*, (1995), Dorset, England, Element Books Ltd.

Patterson, R., *Moon Magic,* (2014), Hants., England, John Hunt Publishing.

Ronner, J., E., *Know Your Angels: The Angel Almanac with Biographies of 100 Prominent Angels in Legend and Folklore – and Much More!*, (1993), Tennessee, USA, Mamre Press.

Stein, D., *Psychic Healing with Spirit Guides and Angels,* (1997), California, USA, Crossing Press.

Tolle, E., *A New Earth; Create a Better Life*, (2009), London, England, Penguin.

Virtue, D., *The Angel Therapy Handbook*, (2011), London, Hay House UK Ltd.

Virtue, D., *Healing with the Angels: How the Angels Can Assist You in Every Area of Your Life*, (2006), London, Hay House UK Ltd.

Virtue, D., *The Lightworker's Way; Awakening Your Spiritual Power to Know and Heal,* (2010), London, Hay House UK Ltd.

Walsh, B., *Advanced Psychic Development*, (2007), Hants., England, John Hunt Publishing.

CPSIA information can be obtained
at www.ICGtesting.com
Printed in the USA
BVHW03s1602160418
513519BV00012B/131/P